A Policeman's Lot

A Policeman's Lot

John Tinnion

A Policeman's Lot
John Tinnion

Published by Aspect Design, 2022

Designed, printed and bound by Aspect Design
89 Newtown Road, Malvern, Worcs. WR14 1PD
United Kingdom
Tel: 01684 561567
E-mail: allan@aspect-design.net
Website: www.aspect-design.net

ISBN 978 912078-37-0

To my wonderful, long-suffering wife, Angie; my equally long-suffering son, Carl and daughter, Stacey, and all other long-suffering spouses, partners and childern who have, and are, carrying out the lonely home 'night shift' while the British streets have, and are, being nobly protected by blue uniform.

This book was written for my amazing grandchildren: Alanah, Gabriel, Rhys, Myoriee, and Elijah.

Contents

Acknowledgements

My grateful thanks go to so many people who, without whose help, this book would not have been written.

Bill Buchan, Father Ian Corbett, and my publishers, who have read my draft, corrected, suggested and invaluably encouraged me throughout the process.

My childhood mates like Paul, Doug and Maureen who made up my music group The Four Squares and set my foot on the right road.

All my early police work mates back in the late sixties in the Met like Allan Holland and Russ Sinton who, unknowingly, set the scene for what you are about to read. (Not to mention those on the other side of the fence who made our lives so interesting and without whose help we wouldn't have had a job!)

But more importantly to those I pestered for years to write books, particularly my son, Carl, whom I unmercifully 'bludgeoned' because I knew he had so many stories within him from his multitudinous travels abroad with YWAM (Youth with a Mission) not to mention his poetry, cooking and art; my late father-in-law, who was a Desert Rat in the war; my own dad who had been a troop train fireman on the railways; our Beauchamp neighbours, all of whom have over ninety years of real-life stories buried within them that need recording. Then I realised—what about me? Put your pen where your mouth is Johnny boy! Hence *A Policeman's Lot*.

There are so many more people too numerous to mention that

I want to thank, that without whose help and input into my life I would not have been moulded into the person I am today. I am privileged to have known these people, had them impact my life and now be fortunate enough to say a huge thank you to them for that input. I sometimes wish it was possible to go back and shake them all by the hand and then realise, in too many cases, it's too late. So often life roars on and we miss those little, but life-changing experiences that I have now been fortunate enough to remember in the recounting of these stories for my book. It has made me realise that we only travel this way once. Life is not a dress rehearsal but the real thing. What we do, think, and say now, is done, thought and said for eternity, and it's sometimes good to just take the time to sit down, meditate and think 'Is there anything I have left undone that can still be sorted? Are there people who are still around today that it's possible to go to and shake by the hand and say, "Thank you"?'

If you're one of those people reading this book, please accept my metaphorical handshake and huge 'Thank you' for being who you are and not even realising you impacted my life in the way you did.

Preface

Not having written a book before, I realise now how proper writers must find it difficult simply knowing where to start! I had made all my notes and written down all the story headers, but now I must fill in the gaps and make it interesting.

Actually, the police force was always interesting for me, sometimes funny, sometimes terrifying, sometimes boring, sometimes very cold and wet, but always interesting . . . in the widest meaning of the word. I hope you will find it as enthralling reading it as I have living it.

So, where to start? Someone once said, the beginning is as good a place as any: I was born at a very early age in Carlisle, Cumberland—and you can't get more 'beginning' than that!

Cumberland, without doubt, is God's own country; lakes, mountains, sea, sand, fresh air, and probably one of the greatest football teams in the English leagues. Some may feel differently, but to me the Blues—Carlisle United—with my childhood heroes Hughie McIlmoyle and Chris Balderstone, were quite honestly the best, and still are. I had great parents, a terrific circle of friends, and a wonderful childhood, in fact, I can't honestly think of any negatives. I went to Carlisle Grammar School, played clarinet with the Carlisle Youth Orchestra, and was in a group at our church called The Four Squares. I was the clarinettist together with Maureen on the piano, Paul on rhythm guitar, and Dougie on bass.

It was the early sixties and I really believe that if the Beatles hadn't got there first . . . they would have struggled to catch us up. But they did get there first, and the rest is history as they say! I swam for Cumberland and Westmorland and was short-listed for the 1964 Tokyo Olympics when I was twelve, would you believe—I'm not sure what brought that encouraging career to a halt more, training ten times a week or getting interested in young ladies—whatever, I didn't go to Tokyo! I was in the rugby first fifteen; athletics for Carlisle, etc.

So why leave it, I hear you say, and why the police? Good questions! Well, academia and me . . . I'll probably just leave it at that! Latin lasted half a term, French five years, and then they wouldn't allow me to sit the O-level—15 per cent in my mocks! (Of course, that was just languages, which were all foreign to me anyway!) Rugby, swimming, and athletics were much more interesting and were apparently of far more importance to the school than lessons (well it often put the school, and the headmaster, in the newspaper and hence had me in the school's good books). Sports made me feel special when I was mentioned in assembly and had my picture on the board, etc. . . . but there was no time for study. Hence, I only passed four O-levels so Oxford missed out and the police won.

I'm not saying I was thick, and that only the police would take me, if that's what you're thinking . . . My interests were peeked mainly because of a careers convention at our school.

I met a policeman who sold it to me, saying that a sportsman in the police force was worth his weight in gold, travelling the world with his given sport for starters, and that if I could also play the clarinet, well, I could become a band member for my whole career and never go on the street! It just sounded like a terrific way to make a living . . . Or he was just very good at his job?

There were a few other things that tipped it for me, of course, but none more so than my rugby-playing school mate who, unlike me, had long wanted to be a policeman and totally won me over too! It seemed like a good idea for us both to 'hit the big time with the men in blue' together! What a team we'd make! It was *fait accompli*!

Having once decided that this was the career for me; the next question was where? Our next door neighbour had been a commissioner of police in Lagos and, after picking his brains, it became apparent that if I intended to 'get on' in the police, I would need to join a large force rather than the small local one. Liverpool and Manchester were suggested, but, if I was going to leave home, I might as well join the world's greatest force, the Met! My apologies to any reader, in or out of the blue uniform, who might think otherwise, but it was to the Met I went.

Of course, interviews, physicals, police entrance exams and the like followed, but not for the police force to start with—the cadets. Well I was just seventeen, in fact sixteen, when I started the ball rolling, but two years of training in preparation for the police sounded like a great idea to our neighbour, to Mam and Dad (well not sure about Mam—losing a fledgling and all that!) and to me. Exciting or what? London! Bright lights! Going to bed when I felt like it! Freedom! Money to burn! Surprising how things turn out.

The interviews, etc. were no picnic, I must admit. Maths, English, geography, current affairs . . . I'd left school to get away from all this and here I was right back in the middle of it, exam paper after exam paper. Then there was the physical—I remember the doctor checking places I didn't even know I had places! Then fitness, the only one I felt okay with, but that was followed by . . . the Hit Squad.

The culmination of all the aforementioned was the interview! Three of the hardest, fiercest, and most frightening men it had ever been my misfortune to meet! I suppose they were only doing a job, but to an innocent sixteen-year-old . . . I haven't a clue what questions they asked or what answers I gave, but it must have been okay, as a little while later the letter came. Success! I was in. I'd been selected as one of six who had been successful out of forty-three applicants!

It was two or three days later that my mate got his results. Now it's worth picturing my mate, he'd been shaving since he was twelve, (I'd only just started); was built like a brick toilet; had the strength of ten horses; hairs on places I still had to invent; the type that would put fear into any self-respecting yob in a heartbeat . . . and he failed. Yes, *failed*!

I was devastated! All my visions of our London high life went up in smoke! I was going to be alone in the big bad city! Apparently, he'd had only 6:5 vision. And in those days, it had to be 6:6 or out.

So my life had come to the inevitable Y-junction. One of those life-changing decisions that actually we meet daily. Sometimes so insignificant that we don't even notice we have altered course, and yet our lives will never be the same. Those times we sometimes look back on and say, 'What if I'd taken the other turn?'

This wasn't a little decision, of course. It was huge, but it still meant that my life was to alter course for ever. The boy was going; those carefree childhood days were soon to be no more, and I would be facing . . . what? I wasn't sure. Initially it was a lark—unreal. An adventure my mate and I were supposed to have had before returning to the warm fold of a secure home in which all harsh decisions would be made by my dad—except that I wouldn't be returning—I was leaving. Those harsh decisions would now be mine to make. Together with the bills!

I remember Dad once describing a Y-junction in his own life: should he remain as a fireman on the railway? Firing those huge steam engines between Carlisle and London Euston. He was almost at a point where he was to be promoted to actually driving one of those gargantuan monoliths—every boy's dream. Or should he go into business as a wholesale potato merchant? Give up a secure job with pay every week for one with no security whatsoever with a young wife and me as a totally dependent six-month-old to support?

He told me he'd always fancied being his own boss, but this was a huge decision to make—so many responsibilities. Which way to go? He said he had felt like a bird in a darkened room flying round in a panic when it suddenly hit black curtains—not a wall. He'd made a decision and the curtains parted for him, the dark room disappeared and he found himself flying high in the air—mountains, streams, and fields carpeted with wild flowers. It wasn't always like that, of course, but he never looked back.

Now it was my turn. A decision had to be made. I couldn't sit at the Y-junction for the rest of my life. Stay or go?

I've got to admit, in a sense, it was a bit of a no brainer. A huge opportunity had presented itself. I'd successfully negotiated a quite stringent entrance programme, and an adventure stood large, inviting, and exciting before me. The dark curtains had opened and revealed a wonderful country vista. I was about to fly into the far blue yonder . . .

Part One

Foot Duty

Chapter One
The Far Blue Yonder!

I was a panda driver, and it was around 2.30 am on a cold, very cold, February morning. Very little was happening, and although we were supposed to be single-manned, I'd picked up a mate to keep me company— and him warm!

We'd talked all the usual talk between young blokes: money (or lack there of), women, beer, etc. when the R/T (radio transmitter) burst into life! Our police station's CID car was chasing a Ford Escort through the flats off East Street. We were in East Street! And from their description, only a few blocks away.

I took the first turning into the flats and hearing the names of specific houses, twisted my way towards the action.

'Decamped!' barked the radio. 'On foot, one white male, approx. six-foot, slim build with jerkin and jeans, heading for Smith House.'

We were at the other end of Smith House, we stopped the panda and jumped out. Alan was going to the left and myself to the right. It was quite dark, the only illumination coming from somewhat poor lights on posts or attached to the house.

I could hear someone shouting 'Stop!' and footsteps running towards me. Out of the gloom I saw a tall male, approximately the right height, tearing towards me. I couldn't miss him, and he appeared to not have seen me. He was only twenty to thirty feet away and heading straight for me at full pelt.

I shouted 'Stop!' He was quite obviously not going to obey my lawful order so, side stepping slightly to my left to give myself a better swing at his solar plexus I delivered the mother of all hay makers. Mohammed Ali would have been proud of me! The snag was, milliseconds before the stroke landed, I heard a little voice shout, 'No, I'm CI——' too late, connection was made and he went down like a sack of potatoes. Wrong bloke, one of the good guys. Well, he didn't get CID out fast enough.

Not my finest hour. Fortunately, Alan had had more success and arrested the right man. I saw my CID colleague in the canteen later. He was okay; sore, well maybe more than sore, but okay. How he'd ever got up from my connection I'll never know — obviously made of stern stuff!

* * *

I'm sure many people who have joined or wanted to join the police force have imagined they would immediately jump into a high-powered police car and roar off after some heinous offender, or leap onto a majestic, shining equine friend and trot around Westminster, accepting the desiring looks of ladies (or gentlemen!) from all walks of life. Maybe even hear those historic words, 'It's a fair cop, guv!' as they apprehend Moriarty moments before Sherlock Holmes! It didn't take long for the truth to dawn . . . I had a little work to do before that! In fact, a lot of work to do!

All policemen must first complete a two-year probationary period, during which they are watched, checked, taught for a couple of days bi-monthly, and basically learn the tools of the trade—and believe me they are numerous! And, of course, all that only follows a thirteen-week training school experience (at least it was thirteen weeks for me back in the late sixties), which was absolutely essential to hopefully turn a wet-behind-the-ears schoolboy into a pillar of society—the Man in Blue.

For me, this training was further proceeded by two years as a police cadet. A period of being a schoolboy-soldier-cum-policeman. Really neither one thing nor another! A transition, I suppose, from a care-free world into a reality of some sort—being bounced round a parade square by a would-be-if-I-hadn't-missed-the-mark sergeant major! Schoolboy lessons in maths, English, modern history, and public affairs mixed with self-defence training and physical exercise that had been designed for the SAS plus . . . long story . . . maybe for another telling!

Just to put that period of my life into more perspective, a typical period in the gym would start with a warm up exercise of bunny hops in pairs down our driveway with a telegraph pole on our shoulders—bunny hops were carried out down on our haunches and the driveway was one mile long! Believe me, the lesson was all down-hill from there. Those PTIs were either sadists from hell or had something seriously wrong with them! For example, one of our first days in the gymnasium these PTI-cum-sadists decided to try us out with free swings on the high bar!

Let me try to draw a picture: no doubt you've all seen gymnastics in the Olympics and our heroic men and women swinging on high-bars? It may seem (and look) so simple . . . Well, believe-you-me, it isn't! I don't know how the coaches teach their wannabes how to swing, but a pound to a penny it wasn't like our PTIs!

I was asked to stand on a stool, lean forward and hold the high bar. My PTI said, 'When you're ready, step off the stool and swing backwards and forwards to get the feel of the motion.'

Obedient, and fool that I was, I did as I was told.

The friction between bar and hands, was intense, nay horrendously painful, and I immediately let go.

The PTI ran to me and said, 'Are you okay?'

I just stared at my hands.

I'd had blisters before but these . . . ! The blisters had formed, ripped off, probably blistered again, and ripped off again! Four on each hand, traffic-signal-red and steaming!

The PTI grabbed my hands and shouted 'Pinkies' at the top of his voice. The other PTIs all came running. My PTI gently held my hands and said, 'This often happens. Don't worry. They'll be okay in a minute.' At which point he produced a bottle of surgical spirits, tenderly looked in my eyes and poured it over my hands!

My first reaction was one of, 'How thoughtful, it's so cool.' The thought lasted all of a nano second before my brain exploded.

I leaped in the air, sent the PTI backwards off his chair, together with his surgical spirits, stool, and all. Grasping my hands, I didn't know whether to scream, laugh, or cry. My brain had left me to fend for myself! Slowly the pain subsided. The PTI looked at me and said, 'Okay now?'

I'd never been in this situation before. I wasn't sure how to react. This guy would probably hold my life in his hands for the next twelve months! All I can remember was looking at him, I mean really looking at him (probably something like a calf would look at the vet after he'd been gelded!) I said nothing, but must have transmitted a lot. I mean, if looks could kill—he was a dead man.

I was sent to the first aid room, treated, and sent back.

My 'mentor' looked at me and said 'Okay?'

'Absolutely,' I lied . . . Nothing more was ever said but somehow, I think, we may have had an understanding. Anyway, thinking about it now, I'm still here, in one piece, and suffering no ill effects. Building moral fibre, I think they called it.

I remember another instructor from those days saying, 'It's all for your own good 'cause it won't look too good if the first time you get into a rough house, or someone on the street calls you a name you won't find in a dictionary you burst into tears!'

* * *

I remember my first morning in Costner Street Police Station, south-east London, walking through the door with my freshly bulled boots, razor sharp creases in my trousers, hair clipped beautifully (even if I do say so myself), and taking my place on parade with my new shift colleagues to be introduced by 'We have a new member on the shift today and he'll buy everybody a coffee . . . if you can pick him out!'

As with all societies, there is a mix of people. The good, the bad, and the downright ugly. (That went for my shift as well as the people we protected!)

I was partnered with George for that first 2—10 shift. A nineteen-stone, five-foot-ten, ruddy-faced, friendly, twenty-three-year service man who had certainly been there, done it, and got the t-shirt! I couldn't have been partnered with a better officer for my first tour. He certainly wasn't built for speed, but what he lacked in that area he more than made up for with experience and good old-fashioned common sense, proving that brains will always win over brawn. Much of the advice I received from him was to stay with me throughout my thirty years of service, and probably the reason why I only ever experienced one serious rough house in all that time.

I was full of adrenaline as we set off on what, for George, was just another tour of duty, but for me—my first! What would happen? I could hardly contain myself.

Around 3.00 pm, a distraught-looking gent ran from the other side of the road, straight in front of a number twelve bus. He had obviously had something very important to tell us and had forgotten there was a road between himself and us! Fortunately, the conscientious and ever-aware London bus driver managed to brake in time. Severely! To the detriment of his passengers! I tried to ignore the fact that a little boy in the process of eating an ice-cream deposited the major contents of his cone all over himself and the back of the elderly lady in front! The bus drove off and left us with the anxious, trilby-hatted gent.

'There's a fight at the Dog and Duck! Someone's going to get killed!'

George thanked him and sauntered on.

I was a little aghast at his nonchalant attitude. Bearing in mind I'd just finished an intensive thirteen-week training course covering everything I would ever need to know about street police work . . . including taking witness statements. Names and addresses at the very least! George simply ignored all protocol and sauntered on.

It was as if someone had just dropped two spoonsful of Epsom salts into my stomach, which had gone off like a fifth of November firework! That, together with the overdose of adrenalin, had me bouncing on the spot in an attempt to get to this fight before 'someone was killed'!

'Come on, George. We'd better step on it. Where's the Dog and Duck?'

In his best Cornish drawl he said, 'It's okay, laaad. Plenty of time.'

The Epsom was really starting to take effect! My first major crime and I was missing it! I tried to calm the buzz-cum-whoosh in my stomach to little effect . . . but every time I tried to speed old George up, he simply replied, 'Not yet, laaad.'

Some ten minutes later we arrived at the corner around which we'd find the Dog and Duck. I tried to dash round but was firmly grasped and dragged back by George who said, 'Me first, laaad.'

He poked his head around the corner, looked for a second and, turning back to me said, 'Give it a minute, laaad.'

I almost exploded! Give it a minute! It had already taken ten to get to this point! By the time we got there, I was sure there'd be bodies everywhere!

George looked again, then turned to me and said, 'Okay, laaad. Slowly does it. Now we can go.'

Still holding my arm to stop me tearing round there, we negotiated the corner.

I was still trying to psych myself up for all the blood and gore, but to my surprise I saw one man flat out on the floor attempting to get up and failing. While the other, totally exhausted, sat with his back to a lamppost.

George approached, surveyed the two of them, then calmly turned to the man who I now know was the landlord and said, 'Okay, Sid, ring the nick. Two to carry in.'

George looked at me, unruffled and calm, slapped me on the back and said, 'Good job, laaad.'

My boots were still bulled, the creases were still in my trousers and I wasn't even out of puff! Big lesson learned.

It reminded me of Jack Reacher, a tough Army M.P. in a Lee Child book I'd enjoyed, who had rotated through an army fight school where the toughest instructor liked to say, 'The best fights are the fights you don't have. No risk of defeat, no risk of injury.'

Cheers, Jack! Cheers George!

* * *

It was around 8.00 pm and right in the middle of 'grub' time, I had a wonderful hand of cards and, for once, thought I might just stand a chance when the station sergeant came into the canteen stating that a local villain was causing a disturbance in his flat.

This sort of call could mean almost anything from a husband-and-wife dispute to a too-much-alcohol party that had taken a wrong turn, to much worse. On this occasion, it was much, much worse!

I was still learning the ropes from George and occasionally going out on my own, but definitely realising every day just how green behind the ears I was. I was trying hard to keep my eyes and ears open, but my mouth shut!

On this occasion, seeing George, together with three other dyed in the wool, older PCs rising, with around seventy to eighty years' service between them—I realised this call was in the latter category, i.e. the much, much worse one!

A fifth PC, whom I didn't know very well, except that he maybe had ten minutes longer than me in the job, also got up to go with us.

Six officers in all, plus a van driver—probably said everything I needed to know. This was going to be interesting!

The 'gentleman' concerned lived off East Street, on the third floor of a quite notorious block of flats, together with his wife. I didn't know him, or anything about him, but the others obviously did. But . . . I knew the flats!

* * *

Before I continue, it might put things into perspective better if I were to relate how I knew the flats. I had been told that this was a block that was never to be entered alone, if it was absolutely necessary to enter it, you should at least be doubled up. Best scenario—go mob handed! I remember thinking to myself at the time, 'I'm a police officer, a member of Her Majesty's Constabulary, with the full weight of the law behind my every action! Who would dare argue with such a person? How bad can any situation be that would mean turning to these lengths? Doubling up! Mob-handed indeed!'

I can remember leaving the nick that day determined to prove the powers that be wrong, and that I was able to control any circumstances that could come my way. What was the worst that could happen? I took a deep breath and turned into the street.

I don't think I'd gone a dozen steps when a bottle of milk smashed inches from my right boot. A full bottle of milk! My initial thought was, 'That was dangerous. Fancy putting a full bottle of milk on a window sill that could be knocked off, crash to the street, and smash! Someone could have been seriously injured!'

I looked at my milk-and-glass-bespattered leg thinking, 'If I don't get this milk off soon, it'll stink' and started to walk off. At this point, my helmet landed at the other side of the road! A crack shot with a bar of soap had done the deed!

All my birthdays came at once, as I realised, 'The powers that be hadn't been joking! Best scenario—Go mob-handed!'

I didn't need a second telling and rapidly found myself several streets away, in a much quieter neighbourhood!

* * *

Well, here I was again. Mob-handed this time! It was my first visit back to the block since the milk and soap episode. This time, although pitch black, I thought, 'I shall be much more vigilant . . . and let the others go first.'

We entered the stair-well of the block to find no lights. Probably due to there being no bulbs in the fittings. One of the PCs suggested we should watch our step, because there was likely to be 'much unpleasant detritus underfoot.' I rapidly found out what detritus was as I immediately slipped on a skin of some sort, tripped over a bag of some sort, and stepped in something that squished and gave off a noxious aroma. This wasn't a 'squishy thing of some sort', I knew exactly what it was. (Why is it always worse to get off than chewing gum?) At this point I hadn't even started to climb the stairs and there were three floors to go.

After much more 'detritus', we arrived at the flat.

The PC I didn't know with ten minutes more service than me—and who had obviously not had the expertise of a George during his two-week street training—removed his truncheon and started to bang on the door with it!

Seeing the seventy to eighty years' of experience take a step back, I thought it sensible to do likewise! It took only seconds for the 'knock' to be answered!

The door swung wide, and almost off its hinges. There in the space now provided stood . . . something. Silhouetted against the room's light stood a man, I presume it was a man, of some nine feet at least, in his underpants, legs akimbo, and covered completely in hair! Not one ounce of fat, just hair and muscle.

The young sprog with ten minutes more service than me stood with truncheon in hand and, for some reason, was speechless. There was also a very strange smell in the air—which was not due to the 'detritus' in which I had stepped—coming from his direction. This could have been because the apparition in front of us had, raised in his right hand, an axe!

George was first to step forward and, acting as if he was delivering a letter, said, 'Hi, Bert. What's up?'

George never ceased to amaze me! It completely defused the situation. Bert, obviously a long-lost buddy of George, simply lowered his axe and stood aside with, 'Hi, George. Come in.'

Apparently Bert's wife had thrown his dinner at him—never did find out why—which had started their obviously noisy and unsavoury discourse. Bert hadn't been too happy about it either, nor were his neighbours. Hence why we had been called.

The 'Far Blue Yonder' was not getting any bluer! Exciting! Different! But Bluer?

Chapter Two
All Alone!

Two weeks later after the Dog and Duck incident was my first morning on my own. George had been great, and I knew he would continue to be so, but this was now the big time! I was on my own! Sink or swim.

His last words to me were murmuring through my head, 'It doesn't matter whether you have twenty days or twenty years as a policeman, when you turn up at an incident; you're the man in blue; the one with the big hat. People will step aside and let you take over. Regardless of what it is. From a cat stuck up a tree to a mangled body lying under the wheels of a lorry. They trust you to know what to do. Regardless of whether you do or not! You're the representative of Her Majesty's Government. They're paying your wages!'

The words were like a river in flood. Fantastic, never-to-be-forgotten words but which, at that moment, were actually covering me with the flood water, plus its mud and silt. Nothing was in view, only thick, muddy water. Everything I'd ever learned . . . buried.

What if I got it wrong? What if I didn't know what to do? What if I looked stupid? What if . . . What if . . . What if? I was about to find out. In trepidation, I donned my helmet and stepped out into the street.

It was 6.00 am. Hopefully nothing would happen. Only cleaners were around and surely they wouldn't be needing anything from me. Well they didn't; but an articulated lorry driver did. I was still in my trepidation aura, when a voice from the ether called, 'Excuse me, Officer. Could you tell me where Wells Street is, please?'

I turned round to see who was speaking and saw the driver leaning out of his cab. I further turned round to see who he was speaking to before I realised it was me!

A thousand things rushed through my head in that instant. 'It's me. I'm the "Officer". I must look like one! It might only be my first day, but he doesn't know, and he's not bothered. He's lost and he's asking me for help. I know the street, and I can help him. This is what I joined up for—helping people!'

'Of course, sir.' Puffing myself up to my full five-foot-ten and a fag paper, I wandered over to his cab.

'If you take the next turning on the left and then second right at the pub,' and in my most important and eloquent, north-country accent, I elucidated the route to him. With a huge smile and generous thanks, he drove off, a very happy man.

I felt like King Kong ... for approximately ten seconds! I'd told him to take the first left! It should have been the first right! I took the mick out of people who got their left and right mixed up, and I'd just done it. Where had I sent him?

The truth slowly dawned on me; first right, then first left was okay but after that ... I'd just sent a forty-foot artic down one of the narrowest streets in S.E. London! Not only that, but there was no turning and it was a dead end!

Frantic, I ran after him and tried to stop him before it was too late.

I never found him! Either he was as bad as me with his left and right, or he'd forgotten what I told him, or he was stuck down a dead-end street! May be he still is!

Dear Driver, if you're reading this today, *please* accept my most sincere apologies! I tried to put it right—honestly.

It's incidents like this that slowly bring you down to earth; set your feet solidly on *terra firma*! It was fortunate that this incident was only to a poor unsuspecting lorry driver, and not something really serious! Well, it was serious to the lorry driver, but you know what I mean.

It was later that day that I was walking along Albany Road, aiming for sixteen beat, the furthest beat from the police station—two to three miles!—when I heard what I at first thought was someone shooting a Tommy gun. I rapidly thought, 'Stupid person! Who has a Tommy gun these days?' I was beginning to think, 'I think too much!' But the sound continued. 'If it's not a Tommy gun—what is it?'

It was getting nearer.

It was then that I remembered my Philips Panda. My first motorbike. Well, not exactly a motorbike. It was a 50 cc moped, but it was all mine and it felt like a motorbike to me. It just didn't sound like one! My mate had a good idea for making it sound like a 650 though. He said that if I loosened the little plate on the bottom of the silencer, stuffed a rag in and then tightened it up, it would sound like a 650! I believed him and it did . . . until the following day when it caught fire!

Gullible was probably a good word! But this noise now approaching me was reminiscent of my Philips Panda, except it was multiplied twenty-fold!

Around the corner came an old Ford Thames van. I use the word 'old', probably 'ancient'—even 'belonging to Adam'—would be better, and quite obviously it had no silencer. Even I knew this was an offence! Trouble was, I had to stop it. This meant stepping into the road and giving a clear raised hand stop signal to the driver!

I'd never done it before. It was my first day on my own. What if he didn't stop? What if he knocked me over because I couldn't get out of his way quick enough? What if it wasn't an offence anyway? What if . . . ? What if . . . ? I was getting fed up with 'What ifs'.

I stepped out, raised my hand, clearly and concisely, text book fashion; probably, if the truth be known, I kept my eyes shut and prayed that he would stop. To my amazement, he did! I directed him to the side of the road, phrasing the first question in my head as I did so, when he said, 'What's up, mate?' As friendly and innocent as you like.

In the driver's seat was a male, not much older than myself, who could hardly see over the steering wheel. 'Take charge of the situation!' I could hear my instructor saying, 'You're the policeman!' It was alright for him to say. He wasn't standing in front of a motorist with a duff exhaust pipe and an accelerator under his foot! It is an offence, and it is against the law! I thought, 'You've got to pull yourself together. This is your job. You have thirty years of this left to do!'

I asked him to climb out of his car, all five-foot-five of him, and in my best police-ish accent, I pointed out the offence to him and cautioned him, completely by the book, and started to write out an HORT 1 (a police document for production of driving documents). I was amazed how rapidly I was falling into the role. Chatting away to him. Him chatting away back. All very nice and friendly, when I happened to notice the car registration number on his road fund licence was different to the one on his car!

''Allo, 'allo, 'allo,' I thought. It was amazing how such an innocuous statement jumped into my head. Where had I heard it before? 'There's something not right here!'

I pointed this out to him, to which he put his hands in the air and said, 'It's a fare cop, guv.'

Those were his very words! I never thought anybody ever said that. But on my first day!

As we continued to chat, the whole story came out. He'd only just bought the vehicle. Hadn't managed to get it insured. There wasn't an MOT for it. He was going to get a driving licence, just hadn't managed yet. On and on went the story, and the offences mounted up. I started to feel sorry for him. Until, while I was looking at his tyres, he tried to run off! Fortunately, I didn't have a problem with fitness in those days—other things maybe, but not fitness—and I managed to catch him within a few yards.

It should be borne in mind, of course, that in those days we didn't have personal radios to call for assistance.

These were the days when the 'Bat Phone' or personal radio had not been invented. (Well, it had been invented, just not supplied to us! Probably because it would have required a wheelbarrow to carry its technology around—how things have changed.)

Information was either disseminated on parade at the beginning of each shift or received on the street by a friendly 'native'. You could also find out yourself from the collator—normally an old PC at the station—who knew everything about everybody and kept a filing system worth its weight in gold. (Not so today, when it's possible to know everything about a vehicle one happens to be following before even stopping it, i.e. name and address of registered owner, whether it's insured, MOTed, taxed, together with anything known about the driver, his friends, things to be aware of, dangers . . . by one simple call over the R/T!)

In those days it took two weeks to find out who was the registered owner! The rest was found out by pure 'sleuthing!'

So here I was, 'sleuthing' finished and only one thing to do— arrest him! He hadn't verified his name and address. The tax disc he admitted stealing from another car, so he needed taking in. Two miles walking! Give or take—but still!

I locked up his van and we walked the two miles back to the

police station. Simple thing to say in one sentence, quite another in reality!

Firstly, as he continually attempted to get away, I had to frog march him. This entailed sticking my hand between his legs from behind and grabbing anything I could get hold of . . . normally the jacket . . . and pulling. You then nudge with your shoulder to ease him off balance, to which he must keep moving his legs forward to stop going base over apex. Also sounds simple until it's attempted in full view of the awestruck public, many of whom would be wondering why a policeman should be sticking his hand between another man's legs! It's quite an exhausting exercise for both parties, especially when carried out for some distance. I was also contending with comments such as, 'Leave him alone, you big bully', 'What's he done?', 'Why are you doing that?' and 'Where are you going?'

Amazing how many inane questions one can be asked! I don't know who was most glad to see the station.

When his vehicle was eventually brought back to the station, I got a traffic specialist in to examine the van for any 'Con & Use' offences—that was vehicle defects against the 'Construction and Use Act', such as tyres, breaks, steering, electrics, etc.

Including the initial offences, he ended up with thirteen in all that day. Turned out to be quite an expensive van!

Things didn't 'crack off', or fall in my lap, every time I left the station!

It wasn't always, 'It's a fair cop, guv!' or 'You caught me hands down!' Sometimes, in fact more than sometimes, I actually had to work for my 'work'. Lots of foot slogging with nothing to show for it. Enough rain water running down the back of my neck to water S.E. London, and even more being sprayed up from cars to wet the bits missed the first time!

It was on one of these 'wandering-around-my-beat-with-not-a-lot-happening' days that I found a black Ford Zephyr parked up outside a block of flats. Nothing too amazing about that I hear you say, except that displayed in the windscreen was a road fund licence with the registration of the car written in pencil, and not written in very cleverly at that! The old number had been rubbed out to such an extent that the perpetrator had almost rubbed through the paper.

Fraudulent use of a road fund licence. Another one! A lot of people were at it, but didn't always get caught, and here I was with two in as many weeks! Tax was expensive, even back then, but there were other reasons: for example, you needed insurance and an MOT to obtain one, or it was a stolen car which had been 'rung' (had had false plates put on it to hide its true identity) and so on.

Which was this? It was parked correctly and was obviously being used. In fact, as I put my hand on the bonnet to examine the tax more clearly, I found it still warm. Used recently!

I hid behind a lamppost just in case I was being observed and contacted my sergeant at the station.

'Keep out of the way, and I'll send a car for you to do some *obs* for a while. You never know, he may be back soon.'

I mean, this was a big job. To me, anyway, particularly with all my minutes of service. Had to be an Old Baily job at least, didn't it? Plus, it was almost booking off time, so there was going to be some overtime. I wasn't doing it for that of course (!) but it always came in handy for a down at heel bobby, eh?

The plain CID car duly arrived. Plain because a panda would stick out like a sore thumb, obviously, and we wanted to be as covert as possible, so we parked unobtrusively nearby, with a clear view of the Ford.

It was around 1.30 pm, lovely day, not too salubrious an area unfortunately, but it was warm and the birds were singing as we settled down for our, who knew how long, vigil.

About three minutes!

We had hardly had time to switch the engine off when a middle-aged guy, as broad as he was tall, returned and put his key in the lock.

''Allo, 'allo 'allo,' I said, well actually I didn't, but the situation definitely lent itself to it.

'Hello, sir. Is this your car?'

I said the guy was as wide as he was tall, and at around five-foot-ten, close up, he was big. Brick toilets definitely came into it, and I thought, 'If things go south; we're gonna have some fun!'

Nothing of the sort. Absolute gent. 'Yes, I just popped home for some sandwiches.'

Although he was big, this was not his most distinguishing feature. It was his eyes. Large, close together and accentuated by 'pebble-bottom' national health-type glasses. They took over his face!

Unbeknown to us, but as we found out later, his nickname was 'Blind Bob'!

He'd apparently been a get-away driver for the mob, or some such big-time villain crew. On one such occasion, he had been parked outside a bank waiting for his fellow felons to return with the 'swag'. Alarms had started sounding as his mates came bursting out of the bank with their bags of cash. They piled into the car and with doors still in the process of being closed, Bob had hit the throttle hard. Flat to the floor, straight into a lamppost. Hence, Blind Bob.

This arrest was a little bit of a come down for him, but nonetheless, he ended up back in court. And we did make some overtime!

Chapter Three
Miracles Do Happen (Even to Policemen!)

Although my first day had been quite eventful, life started to get onto a much more even keel as I started to settle into my role as a beat man at Costner Street Police Station.

We used to have six weeks of early and late shifts, week about, followed by three weeks of nights. Pretty horrendous when I look back, rising at 4.30 am for a 6.00 am early shift. Going to bed after midnight following a late shift. Enduring the quick change over from late to early, i.e. going to bed around 1.00 am to be rising at 4.30 am for the next shift, or the even worse change over from nights to lates, going to bed around 7–8.00 am and back on at 2.00 pm. The old body (well nineteen-year-old body then!) took some hammering on that one. It just didn't know which way was up! It took nearly three weeks for the body clock to get into sync with nights—and then—back to days with very little sleep at that, as it thought it was time to go to bed at 1.00 pm rather than get up . . . even now my brain gets confused . . . (as no doubt yours is after that explanation!).

Somehow as nineteen and twenty-year-olds, it didn't matter. The shift was your mates, your social life. We went to the pub together, to parties together. Supported each other during urgent assistant shouts when a colleague was in a sticky situation.

It was common place to go to parties during early turn week and not go to bed! How we did it, I haven't a clue, but it was great fun!

It was one such time that found Al and me somewhere between Croydon and Brighton at 2.00 am with a broken fan belt—and early turn looming at 6.00 am!

We'd been invited to a nurse's party in Penge. Nurses' parties were always good fun. Possibly because we sung from the same hymn sheet—shift work, dealing with people from all walks of life—similar lifestyles. During the evening we got lucky (is that the correct terminology?), we met two lovely young ladies with whom we got on very well.

Around 1.00 am, we realised the party was slowly coming to an end, but our friendship wasn't. The girls were friends and had come together to the party in Charlie's car. Charlie being the lady with whom Al had struck up a liaison. None of us wanted to say goodnight and so when Sue, the lady with whom I had struck up a liaison, suggested we go to Brighton for a paddle (as you do!) we all fully agreed.

Charlie wanted to drive, and so we all piled into her Singer Chamois. The Chamois was really a Hillman Imp with a fast back. Very cute, very rare, but very small. As Sue and I were in the back, I wasn't complaining!

Simon and Garfunkel were crooning gently on the radio, and I think Sue and I were coming up for air for maybe the third or fourth time when Charlie announced that her ignition light had come on. In perfect harmony with the radio, Al and I shouted 'Stop!'

Sue jumped out of her skin and Al nearly disappeared through the front windscreen as Charlie slammed on the brakes. I had blown an engine on one occasion by not stopping soon enough when the ignition light came on. Charlie made sure that wasn't going to happen!

We wound ourselves out of the car and lifted the bonnet. It was completely, absolutely, and utterly pitch black. Although it wasn't raining, it was cloudy and therefore there were no stars and no moon. We also happened to be around an hour out of London and an hour from Brighton! Basically, the middle of nowhere.

Neither Al nor I would really have known what to look at in the daylight, let alone in the dark, but we had to appear 'the knights in shining armour', didn't we? Luckily, it didn't need a genius to find the fault: the fan belt was gone! And we *did* know the remedy for no fan belt: a lady's stocking. In those days ladies rarely wore tights— thank goodness. Sue and Charlie obliged, hence we had four, and we dutifully tied the first round the pullies. Within a mile it had snapped. Within three, we'd used them all!

Al and I stared at each other. It was 2.00 am and, as I said, the middle of nowhere. A car that was as rare as hen's teeth, and early turn in was in four hours! We fell apart! The girls couldn't for the life of themselves think what was so funny. Poor Charlie thought her 'baby' was bound for the scrapyard!

Plans had to be made. Where was the nearest garage? How were we to contact one? How were we to get to one? How were we to contact the nick to let them know of our predicament? Should we walk back towards Croydon or on to Brighton and hope for a lift? Which was nearest? No mobile phones in those days!

Whilst contemplating the dilemma, we saw headlights coming towards us! We couldn't believe our luck and as the vehicle approached, we jumped out and waved for all we were worth.

A Triumph TR 6 pulled up and a very smart gent of around forty got out.

'Having a spot of bother, lads?'

To say the least, we thought and explained the situation.

'Hang on a minute,' he said. 'I think I've got a fan belt for the Chamois in the boot.'

Al and I thought we'd misheard him—*for the Chamois*! *In his boot*!

True to his word, he returned in less time than it had taken for the belt to break with a fan belt for the Chamois! We couldn't have been more surprised had he given us four round-the-world air tickets!

He also had a spanner and set about replacing it.

It seemed like seconds later that he closed the boot with, 'There you go, lads.' Got back in his car and drove off! We hadn't even thanked him let alone tipped him. We just stood staring at each other as we saw his rear lights disappearing off towards London. We were probably almost in Brighton before one of us said, 'What just happened?' We thought the best we could have hoped for was a lift to some lights, or a phone box . . . but this!

There's a verse in the bible; Hebrews 13:2 that says, 'Be not forgetful to entertain strangers: for thereby some have entertained angels unawares.'

Utterly amazing and will always remain . . . A miracle!

* * *

We had just finished parade and were ready to start a 'late turn' when the station sergeant approached, 'Hi John. Little Toby Smith's over the wall again. Bound to be back at home. Can you go and pick him up?'

Children, young people, and women were normally dealt with by the women police department—yes, a specific department in those days; the concept of having ladies on the beat and part of the shift had not been invented then. (It's only since then that we have realised what an incredible and necessary addition they are to the police service.) It was inconceivable to think of these 'tender flowers' being out on the street and at the mercy of villains—PCs getting a good pasting while trying to protect the ladies. How wrong could we be . . . ! They have been, and are, a wonderful and necessary part of the police force.

Mind you, I'll never forget being introduced to our WPC Department on my arrival at the station and am quite certain that not a villain, PC, or anyone else would have argued with them had they been out on patrol, particularly as I gazed up into their eyes and had the blood gently extracted through the ends of my fingers as they shook my hand and said, 'Welcome to the team.'

I wish I'd got to know them better as I was later to learn that you really can't tell a book by its cover; each of these three fantastic ladies were real earth mums—professionals to the enth degree and incredible experts in their field—what they didn't know about the Children and Young Persons Act wasn't worth knowing.

I'm certain we not only lost expertise, wisdom, and knowledge when that department eventually closed its doors, but a whole lot more. However, time has shown that what we lost on the roundabouts we gained on the swings.

Little Toby was around nine years old and had been placed in an approved school basically for being 'beyond parental control'— among other things . . .

Approved schools don't exist today, going out after the 1969 Children and Young Peoples Act. I suppose they were one step down from a borstal, which was much tougher as well as enclosed. However, even then, being at an approved school was not terribly pleasant.

Toby was forever 'going over the wall' as we called it, or 'absconding' to use the correct term.

Young coppers like me were normally sent on these jobs, rather than handing it to the WPCYP Department, as it was a good learning ground for dealing with bigger arrests which required, more or less, the same paperwork—so off I set.

Mum, dad, and Toby were no problem. Both mum and dad knew he had to go back and so did Toby. It was a lark to him anyway. He'd have a couple of days away from the 'school' and knew it wouldn't be long before he'd be out again the first chance he got, so—all in all—a win-win situation for all concerned; he had some time at home and I got some paperwork exercise.

The only problem was that he didn't live in the most salubrious of areas—for a start, it was only a stone's throw from the axeman's flat!

Secondly, as I stood in his street considering my next move, I noticed a refrigerated door had lost its owner and was propped up against a lamppost with rancid rainwater pooled in the butter compartment; the dust bins were severely over stocked causing the footpath to be somewhat of an assault course; and several dogs had suffered what appeared to be an excess of curry the night before . . . but . . . it was still a beautiful evening and I refused to allow a few little 'ancillaries' to spoil my mood. It was a typical September day with the sunlight bright and golden, reminding me that summer was rapidly sinking into autumn—with all its glorious colourfulness.

I glanced at the address on my report to check exactly which flat I was going to in the Peabody buildings. The tall, thin, brown brick, turn of the century tenement structure stood forebodingly over me as a dust cart trundled by, adding more noxious aromas to my already overloaded senses. Toby's flat was on the third floor with a staircase very similar to that of our axeman friend. Cans, paper, dustbin contents without dustbins, loo contents without the loo—need I go on?

The door had a doorbell with the button missing—wires sticking through the door jamb—and no knocker. I tapped a couple of times and was rewarded with an immediate response.

The door opened and mum, a thirty-something-year-old lady, with peroxide blonde hair, wearing an apron in desperate need of seeing the inside of a washing machine, tights at half-mast and fluffy slippers with a huge bobble on the front, greeted me with 'Come in, mate. He's here. He'll be ready in a couple of minutes. Just having a glass of pop. Want a cup of tea?'

The room was inordinately hot and had an oddly sweet smell of sweat, and old grease, mixed with cigarette smoke, stale beer, and dog.

Apart from the entrance door, there appeared to be only one other door in the single ten-foot by ten-foot room in which I stood. I assumed it to be the toilet as there was already both a double bed and sink beside me.

Dad was lying in bed, shirtless, among brown-cum-grey-should-have-been-white sheets with three children aged somewhere around three, five and seven. I then noticed number four would be due soon! (I later found out that they all slept head to toe in the one bed—obviously privacy wasn't too high on the agenda.)

I also couldn't help but notice that the threadbare carpet had more grease, bacon rind, and stale chips ground into it than I'd eaten for my dinner. The sink was overflowing with dishes containing the residue of several days' meals gone by, together with nappies, knickers, and socks.

Toby's mum extracted a chipped mug from among the melee in the sink, wiped it on her apron and began to make me a cup of tea.

'That's very kind of you,' I lied, (actually, it wasn't a lie, it *was* very kind of her; it was the next bit that was the lie!) 'But I had one minutes before I came out.'

She dropped it back in the sink, tried to give Toby a bye-bye hug of which Toby was having none of—far too old and macho for that—before tucking his shirt in and handing him over to me.

Dad took another swig from his beer can, belched and laid back down. Never did manage to find out how he could drink

from a can with a fag-end still in his mouth and appear to go back
to sleep with it still lit!

As I stood outside the flat, I looked down at Toby and couldn't
help but wonder, why does this little fellow want to come back here?
What really makes up a 'home'? He was almost certainly in for a
caning on his return (corporal punishment was still very much in
vogue in those days). I'm sure he loved a cuddle from mum—he
just wasn't going to let me see it. It couldn't be the building or flat.
So what was the reason?'

All the old sayings came back: 'home sweet home,' 'there's no
place like home,' 'the best journeys take you home,' 'a house is
made of bricks and beams; a home is made of hopes and dreams' . . .
hundreds of them! But which fitted this situation? Why suffer
a caning on his return to the school—which occurred at least
monthly—to go back to what I had just witnessed?

What had been the norm for me was very different for Toby,
but I suppose what you've never had, you never miss. This had been
all he'd ever known. He obviously got cuddles, and I'm sure love,
from mum, but not a lot else, other than maybe more freedom
than in an approved school? No apparent correct correction. By
that I mean he no doubt received cuffs behind the ear for spurious
reasons (like standing in the way of dad's TV etc!) but, I should
think, no correct instruction.

I suppose home is where your heart is, and Toby's was here. I'm
sure there are psychologists who would have the answers to my
questions and could put these things in perspective, but, standing
there on that afternoon, I was somewhat confused.

* * *

Policework was a good life. No, it was a great life, particularly for
a young adventure-loving bloke like me. Of course, there were
also the becalmed periods when nothing much happened, during
which times you wandered about getting cold or wet, or both, when
sensible people would look for a 'tea hole', or some cosy nook or
cranny where one could get warm and rest the weary feet. (Twenty
story flats had wonderful boiler rooms in the cellars, built, I'm quite
certain, for cold, lonely policemen like me!)

Of course, sometimes none were available, and I would simply
stand in a shop doorway, covered arch or similar, trying to keep
dry, water dripping from my nose and helmet, wondering why I'd
joined the job.

It was on one such occasion that, as I stood by a wall in the
entrance to a lane, I caught my easiest burglar!

It was around 2.00 or 3.00 am that—whilst thinking about
nothing in particular; my brain in neutral and dreaming I was
warmly tucked up in bed—a 'gentleman of the night', better known
as a villain, whose last thought was being tucked up in bed, jumped
over the wall and into my arms!

I don't know who was most surprised, as we stood gazing fondly
into each other's eyes! He with his newly acquired bag of 'trophies'
or me with fading memories of bed!

It was another miracle, or he was the unluckiest thief on the
patch. Either way, it gave me a nice warm ending to the night as I
sat and wrote up my report in the canteen, enjoying a bottomless
mug of steaming hot coffee.

In a similar vein . . . where have you been when you've been
nowhere? And what have you been doing when you've been doing
nothing? On another 2.00 am jaunt along the high street, again
thinking of nothing in particular, I saw a large broken shop window.
Similar to many I'd seen in and around Walworth with a story to

tell, a report to write, and numerous enquiries to be made. But this one was different—there was a leg sticking out of it! The leg was moving and obviously attached, somewhere in the murk of the shop, to a body. Sure enough, the leg was followed by two arms holding a TV (as was to be expected!) and finally the head and body.

As the body fully emerged from the shop, the expression on its face when confronted by me was, without doubt, one to remember.

''Allo, mate,' I said.

No reply. Just a stare.

'Where you been?'

'Nowhere,' it said, finding its voice.

'What you got there then?'

'Nothing.'

'Always wanted to know where *nowhere* was. Let's go to the nick and you can tell me all about your trip.'

I must go down as one of the most fortunate PCs on record. To get such positive results with little or no effort!

Never did find out where *nowhere* was . . .

* * *

A few days later I left the station, I turned into the high street and was confronted by an old Foden tipper lorry, heavily laden with hardcore, struggling under its considerable weight and spewing copious amounts of exhaust fumes into the faces of the shoppers. Some were clearly distressed, others simply accepted it as just another London day at the shops!

To me it was another story. It belonged to a firm I'd reported on several occasions for no road fund licence, no operator's licence, numerous vehicle defects, not to mention driving offenses such as not having insurance, jumping traffic lights, pedestrian crossing violations, no HGV licences held by the drivers, no MOTs—the list was endless. I'd been to the firm's offices (or should I say their shack in a yard!) and reported the owner—but all to no avail, it would appear, as here they were at it again. The strange thing was, I never seemed to get one to court.

I stopped the lorry to find it being driven by a man I'd not seen before, but I went through the usual procedure regardless . . . no tax or operators' licence being displayed, etc., etc., finishing with 'You will be reported . . .'

Deep in my gut I thought, 'I'm wasting my time! Number one, the driver will no doubt disappear into the ether, the owner will do nothing about it, and it won't go to court anyway! Won't go to court anyway! Why?'

As I sat in the canteen writing up the report later that day, the thought *why?* kept going through my mind. Why aren't they going to court. These vehicles are totally illegal and death traps. This firm should be stopped!

I could feel myself getting more and more wound up when a voice from behind me frightened the life out of me; well, certainly, roused me from my thoughts; 'Another good one, I hope, John? You are doing a good job. Catching the right sort of offenders!'

It was my station sergeant.

'Trying, gov,' was about all I could respond.

'So, what's this one then?'

I told him what had transpired, but then, before I could stop myself, launched into my dejection and told him how I couldn't believe these cases weren't going to court.

'Mmm. Let's go to my office.' Was all he said.

* * *

I loved vehicles. Always had. From mopeds to commercial lorries. This love was no doubt birthed in me by my dad who had been a wholesale potato merchant and, as such, needed a lorry to collect the spuds from the farms. He had an old 1948 Dodge flatbed lorry, maximum speed 20 mph (even had to have it displayed on its rear mud flaps) maximum weight it could carry—7 tons. It was his pride and joy until his new one arrived. A 1952 Dodge flatbed!

It makes me feel really old now but looking back . . . they were great. I loved them and spent may happy hours with my dad, washing them, polishing them, riding in them. I can smell the oil in the cab now . . . combined with the diesel fumes (I think more came in the cab from the engine, than went out of the exhaust pipe).

I remember going to Kendal with him on one occasion to collect a load of potatoes from a farm: a matter of around a hundred miles there and back (couple of hours today, if that) but eight hours then! Only the A6, no motorway . . . and Shap . . . a geographical link between the Lakeland Fells and the Pennines. Travelling north on the M6 today, we cross Shap and don't realise we're doing it. Top gear all the way. No extra strain experienced to the engine (unless you happen to be the proud owner of a Citroen Dianne or 2 CV as I was back in the seventies. Wonderful funmobile yet the only one I ever owned that caused me to change gear on any slight rise in the road—on one occasion I was even overtaken by a cyclist! I always wanted a large key welded to the boot . . .). I digress. Pre-motorway days, the hills of the A6 were, and still are, a little more substantial than most, and to lorries like the old Dodge, and even the majority of cars, were a trial!

I can still hear my granddad coming in one night and shouting to my dad with euphoria 'Harry! I crossed Shap in second! Didn't have to drop into first once! These modern cars!' He drove a 1953 Singer!

All this is to say that I had birthed in me in those days a love of vehicles that has transcended time—particularly for HGVs. If I'd ever had the cash, I would have loved to renovate an old lorry, particularly a 2-stroke Commer truck—that engine sound—a hollow, echoey, almost musical pitch that was unlike any other vehicle of its day.

But—and that's a big 'but'—it was an anathema to me to find them not looked after, like this tipper firm character, lovely lorries allowed to go to rack and ruin and become illegal death traps. All their former beauty was lost in grime, rust, and neglect.

'So, none of these particular processes involving this firm have been getting to court, eh?' said the station sergeant.

'I just can't understand it,' said this green as grass rooky!

'From now on, I want you to pass any future processes involving this firm directly to me. Okay?'

'Yes, Sarge,' was all I could think of to say, but I realised I had probably opened a quite substantial can of worms. I never found out how large, but from then on every report went to court.

Several weeks later, I stopped another tipper belonging to this firm. I decided to go to the owner's yard as usual to ensure the firm, as well as the driver, were reported prior to the report being handed in. The yard was in its usual scrap-strewn state, but there was a different atmosphere to it, or at least so it seemed to me. It was another grey, drizzly day but something was different. It wasn't the smell of grease, diesel, or cheap cigar smoke mingled with even cheaper aftershave either.

The owner was smiling. I couldn't believe it, he was even pleased to see me!

'I've got something for you in the office,' he said. 'Got a minute?'

From under his desk he produced . . . a salmon!

It was all I could do to keep a straight face, 'I suggest you

offer it to the judge,' I said and started to make my way back
to my beat.

A dejected look crossed his face, and I almost felt sorry for him.
Almost. My dad had been a businessman and I knew how hard it
was to keep afloat sometimes. However, resorting to bribery was
not just unethical—it was illegal.

'I will report you every time I see one of your lorries on the road
until you sort out your licences, drivers and vehicles. Could you live
with yourself if one of your vehicles was involved in an accident in
which a member of the public was seriously injured or even killed?'

I realised I was starting to preach and left him with an 'I'm
forgetting about the salmon, and hope that next time we meet,
your business will be legal, firmly on the rails, and bringing you in
plenty of cash! This route will very rapidly become very expensive
in the long run.'

Chapter Four
The 'Not-so-Nice' Side

Regrettably, it's inevitable that on occasions, we are called to deal with the more unpleasant side of the job: delivering death messages; being called to suicides; sudden deaths, at home or in the street; having to sit in a burnt-out house all night with its occupant who had failed to get out in time; and so on. None of which tend to lend themselves to particularly good bedtime reading!

However, without being too macabre, the odd story probably needs to be told. One such incident caused me to take my first step into manhood and emphasised my naivety and trust of older PCs whose sole purpose in life seemed to be to harden me up—a learning curve, or so they told me!

It was another occasion when my 'grub-break' was to be disturbed. Two older PCs, with whom I hadn't had many dealings, wandered into the canteen and asked me if I'd ever seen a dead body! It was one of those areas which I knew I would have to deal with at some point, but obviously one I was not relishing. All I'd ever had to deal with was losing my pet rabbit and attending her funeral.

* * *

Actually, I had worked at a frozen chicken factory one summer, during the school holidays, where I'd seen hundreds of dead chickens, but I wasn't counting *them*.) Maybe another quick aside—Chickpac was a factory where live chickens went in at one end and came out frozen in a bag at the other. Being the new boy on the block, the factory workers took it upon themselves to 'initiate' said new boy! (Many tricks were played on me during that sojourn, which I almost took in the right spirit . . . almost.) But one still gives me nightmares.

Part-way round the conveyor belt sat an older gent whose job was to separate the neck from the chicken—they were headless and gutted at this stage, and the neck was needed for the giblet bag—all he had to carry out the task was a pair of secateurs and a very large forearm. His job appeared simple enough, and when he asked me to stand in for him for a second while he went to the loo, I innocently agreed. The first couple of minutes were okay, but rapidly my hand and arm got tired. In fact, it got to the point where I thought my hand would drop off! But the conveyor was a continually moving belt. I desperately looked round for some help, but everyone was engrossed in their own jobs. I couldn't stop without the entire line coming to a stop, and hence the whole factory grinding to a standstill! I should point out that after my station, the bodies of the chickens went into a covered section in which rubber fingers were rotated onto them to remove any last feathers missed at the plucking stage, and then washed with high powered jets of water. My hand had ceased to be part of my body, but I had to keep going. The conveyor seemed to be speeding up and I rose from my seat in an attempt to keep up. But it was no good, I couldn't, and the covered section was looming!

It got to the point where I was almost climbing into the unit; I was soaked to the skin, but the job had to be done. Suddenly, I was aware that the line had stopped, and I was slowly catching up with myself. Exhausted, I thought, 'Thank goodness for that, and with senseless fingers I climbed out of that watery hell. I attempted to continue to cut out the necks . . . Mmmm, slow on the uptake or what!

The entire factory had turned up to watch my débâcle! Ah well, another lesson learned, and they all had a good laugh.

* * *

Back to my story; having fallen foul at Chicpac, I should have realised that this was one of those occasions when beginners in all walks of life must contend with 'jokers'. Pathetic 'jokers'! E.g. 'Can you pop to the stores and ask for a long stand? Ta. And could you bring back a sky hook while you're at it? Oh, and while you're there, I need a left-handed screwdriver.' You know the type!

We arrived at a two-up two-down in the middle of a row of terraced houses where we were told that a large, elderly lady had passed away in the night and needed bringing down the stairs. Arriving in her bedroom I thought how very peaceful she looked, and I thought I'd not needed to worry about how I'd feel.

The PCs with me assessed the situation and told me that as she was going to be very heavy, they would take the head end as that would be considerably heavier than the feet. I thought it a kind gesture and took the feet. They stood back to allow me to go down the stairs first. Approximately half way down I got the 'joke': together with other things I didn't want! The control of her bodily functions was gone . . . Need I say more?

It was a mistake I was never to make again and, incidentally, to try out on anyone else! Without being a stuffed shirt, it may have been their idea of a practical joke, but certainly not mine.

Another somewhat unpleasant episode was to occur on a cold, frosty February morning around 1.00 or 2.00 a.m. The temperatures had to be well below freezing but I must admit, I was as warm as toast, being well wrapped up in my great coat. (The great coat was a uniform issue for which, on nights like these, lonely wandering

PCs were hugely grateful. Goodness only knows what they were made of as they weighed a ton. They were so heavy they literally made my shoulders ache—but, as I said, on a night like this, it was a small price to pay.)

It was one of those crisp, clean, fresh-smelling nights when there were no cars about to pollute the air and I was just about to take a lungful of this rare bounty, when I saw what I thought was a bundle of rags on the pavement a short distance in front of me.

As I approached, I began to realise that something or someone, was inside them. I gently turned them over and saw it was old Bert, a well-known vagrant on our patch. His face was blue-grey with a thin film of frost on it. His body was stiff, probably from excessive exposure to the frosty night, and no wonder, his cloths were threadbare to the extent that his knees showed through his trousers, and his coat, although thick in places, still exposed his skin in others. His shirt had no buttons, and he wasn't wearing a vest. All in all, he obviously wasn't dressed for a night like this, and now, too late, I had discovered his sad, frozen body.

At least he wasn't feeling the cold now, and I had to wonder how this sort of thing could happen in our day and age. Here was a man of around fifty-five to sixty years of age. Young. Ten years short of his three score years and ten. A man who had once had dreams and aspirations. Loving and being loved. To my shame I knew nothing about him. I'd seen him numerous times around the area—shuffling from dustbin to dustbin—sitting on numerous street corners begging for the occasional bit of spare change that the mostly uninterested passers-by would drop in his cap.

As far as I knew his home was under newspapers on any free park bench, a deep doorway, the subway, or, when very fortunate, a police cell after having been arrested for vagrancy or simply being drunk on boot polish or meths.

What could I have done? What could anyone have done? Were there not organisations and charities set up for people just like Bert? Had they failed? Had the system failed? I was pointing a desperate finger at everyone else trying to pass the blame, but found I had three fingers pointing back at me!

Fault didn't come into it. Bert was gone. Nobody was to blame. Everyone was to blame.

It was obvious how Bert had died, but the processes had to be adhered to to ensure that death had been sustained through normal circumstances and not spurious. A doctor had to certify death and I had to stay with the body for continuity of evidence. Staying with the body meant staying with the body! On the street. Transference to hospital. Certification by a doctor. Post mortem. Placement in morgue. Yes, post mortem. Not one of my favourite memories.

The post mortem was simply to verify the cause of death and I remember whilst the process was being carried out, trying desperately to study the ceiling—sometimes the wall in front of me—occasionally the floor! But, of necessity, occasionally I had to look at the proceedings if, and when, the pathologist wanted to draw my attention to something. On one such occasion, the pathologist said, 'Look at that!'

I hadn't a clue to what he was referring and won't give you sleepless nights by telling you what I looked at, but he continued, 'That is the most beautiful aorta I've ever seen. Spotless. Not one iota of fat. That tells me that this man did not die from a heart attack. If I hadn't known he'd been a drinker, I would have told you that he'd consumed copious amounts of cider in his lifetime. Some people say an apple a day keeps the doctor away. I say a cider a day keeps the heart attack away!'

He went on to explain that apparently cider eats fat and that in the olden days when vats of cider were being brewed, the chief brewer would hang a rat in the barrel and when it came out as bones—the cider was ready! All the fat eaten! Apparently today, it's done with hanks of ham. I'm only repeating what I was told, but . . . ! I love a glass of cider, and to think it's so healthy and good for me . . .

* * *

About 2.00 am one morning I was just returning to the nick for some grub and a game of cards, when a young girl of maybe ten or eleven came up to me and said, 'We can't get into Daddy's room.'

Why does everything happen around 2.00 am or just as your about to have some 'tucker'? The lateness of the hour and no mum with her told me it wasn't a normal call for help. Cards and grub would have to wait, and we should get to 'Daddy's room' ASAP!

Their flat happened to be just round the corner and so, five minutes later, I found myself outside 'Daddy's room'.

Mum and grandma were sitting sobbing in the lounge. They just pointed to a door across the corridor and I left the little girl climbing onto mum's lap.

Expecting the worst, I attempted to open the door. It moved a little, but the type of resistance told me that something (or someone) was preventing the door from opening. I pushed harder and the door gave a little. An extra shove and the obstruction was removed. However it wasn't quite as simple as that, or what I was expecting, because what transpired only moments later was that daddy had, in fact, hung himself from a stanchion on a window above the door with his neck tie. My push had only moved the body slightly allowing the gentleman's head to pop round the corner.

Never having been confronted with such a spectacle was, to say the least, a shock. That, coupled with the fact that the face was blue, the eyes protruding and the tongue sticking out, all added to the awe of the moment, and then, thinking that the worst was over, a sudden scream from behind me caused an extremely rapid liquification of my stomach contents. Unbeknown to me the little girl had followed me out and had seen what I saw at the same moment! A heroic act of bodily function control on my behalf saved me from an embarrassing scenario as I gently led her back to her mother.

'Is he . . . ? Is he . . . ?' was all mum could say. I nodded and asked her to keep her now very upset daughter with her. As I wandered back to the bedroom, I thought how incredibly brave the little mite had been. Knowing something was very wrong, to have come to the police station was, in itself, brave, but her whole attitude up to that point had been one of immense 'adulthood', far out-weighing that of her mother and grandmother.

I contacted the station and asked for an ambulance and the duty officer to attend. As I entered the room, I realised the body was still blocking the doorway and needed to be cut down. The only tool I had to hand was a rather blunt penknife. I pulled a chair up and began to saw through the tie.

The gent hadn't been terribly big, eleven or maybe twelve stone, quite slim, (but a 'dead weight' is so termed for a reason) and *rigor mortis* was beginning to set in, therefore attempting to support the body weight with one hand and saw through the tie with a blunt penknife with the other, made me wish I'd waited for help.

Suddenly the material gave way and the feet of the body dropped to the floor. I managed to keep a hold of him, but the extra weight caused a bending of the midriff. In turn, that applied pressure to the lungs thereby expelling air. The air passing over the vocal cords caused a deep moan-cum-growl to be emitted, frightening the life out of me. I literally thought he'd come back to life!

All the horror stories I'd ever read, or films I'd watched, had nothing on this episode, and needless to say, I was delighted when my boss plus an ambulance crew arrived.

It wasn't an experience I wanted to repeat in a hurry, but it was 'just another day' in the life of a beat bobby which continued to add to my life's rich tapestry as I wended my way to the 'Far Blue Yonder'.

Chapter Five
The Ass!

You may have heard the phrase, 'The Law is an Ass!' You may agree with it. You may not. You may not be bothered. You may think, 'I know what I'd call it!'

Having worked at both ends of the spectrum, I'm still undecided. We can probably all tell stories to prove or disprove it. We realise that magistrates and judges have a difficult job to do and that if the evidence is not present, regardless of how guilty the police officer knows the felon to be, he must be released. But when a clever lawyer twists a story or a police officer fails to give—or give correctly—a caution for whatever reason (i.e. difficult arrest, avoiding a knife, avoiding a mob who don't want their mate arrested, stress of the moment, etc.) and—regardless of how compelling the evidence is against the defendant, how serious the crime, or the fact that he may be a prolific criminal—the defendant gets released . . . one must ask . . . 'Really!?'

One such incident was told me in my very early days, it concerned a young couple, let's call them Jack and Jill, who went out for a drink.

It was apparently around nine or ten o'clock and the pub was heaving: raucous laughter, giggling girls, music at full pelt, clinking glasses. A guy, let's call him Buster, walked up to the bar and immediately took a fancy to Jill and started using all his best chat-up lines on her! Jack was a little surprised and, obviously, none too happy. Politely, he asked the newcomer to bog off!

Jack, from what I hear, was a handsome hunk of around six-foot-two, slim but firmly built, and normally of quite a mild character. But when the love of your life is threatened, it's amazing how the red mist comes up, and as Buster was taking no notice of the request, a quite heated discussion began. Buster, a somewhat smaller but very much wider man, and of a more unpleasant nature, promptly produced a knife. Wasting no time, he calmly plunged it into the soft area round the neck, the part immediately behind the collar bone and in front of the epiglottis. The force he used, caused the knife to almost disappear into Jack's body, causing the blade to pierce his heart, killing him instantly. Jack's mate, Bill, horror struck at what he'd just witnessed, jumped up to put his penneth in.

The whole pub was now recovering from the initial shock of seeing such blatant, horrific violence and had jumped up, some to get involved and some to simply get out of there. Not noticing and somewhat unperturbed, Buster removed a cut-throat razor from his pocket and slashed Bill's face into, what has since been described as, ribbons!

Buster, now seeing the crowd, and rapidly realising he was completely outnumbered, decided against trying anymore chat up lines on Jill, ran from the pub . . . and straight into the arms of a passing policeman!

That was basically the nuts and bolts of the story.

Buster was taken to court for murder, GBH (grievous bodily harm) and carrying an offensive weapon. Straightforward, you'd think, pub full of witnesses, etc. But for some reason, known only to the powers that be, the murder and GBH charges were dropped, leaving only the charge of offensive weapon . . . for which Buster received a conditional discharge.

The condition being that he shouldn't carry a knife!

* * *

A few years later a similar, unbelievable case occurred. This time to me. There had been a spate of car thefts in the area. Strange ones that didn't seem to benefit anyone. Cars taken from random streets to remote areas and then set on fire.

Normally cars are stolen to either sell on for a profit, break up into parts which are then sold on, or simply as a means of getting home when Joe Soap misses the last bus and can't be bothered to walk. So, he steals a car and then dumps it. Often cars are burnt out to remove the perpetrator's fingerprints or just because sometimes the thief likes the power buzz he gets at causing such carnage! Watching, as fire gets to the petrol tank and the subsequent explosion, or just simply watching the flames like a dog in front of the hearth. (They say that often dogs can go blind from such a practice as it burns the retina or something—maybe a vet could put me right on that—it would certainly be instant justice if that was to happen to Joe Soap!)

However, at this time, nothing seemed to fit the criteria until one day a stolen car was stopped and was found to be driven by an eight-year-old boy! As the boy was under the age of criminal responsibility nothing could be done except make a report, take the boy home, explain the situation to the parent, and hope parental guidance would take its course.

It turned out this was not an isolated occurrence. As slowly more and more eight to nine-year-olds were stopped driving stolen cars and being found at the sites of burnt-out cars, it was obvious that something else was afoot. The extensive enquiries which ensued revealed that a disgruntled family wanted to get their own back on the police service by attempting to cause as much disruption as was possible.

Actually, it was more a disgruntled fifteen-year-old son of a disgruntled family who took it upon himself to cause the hassle! The son apparently felt that his dad had been hard done by by the police in that he felt he was being singled out, targeted if you like, on too many occasions. He probably thought that dad should be left alone to carry out his burglaries and provide for the family in peace!

He therefore took it upon himself to instruct under ten-year-olds how to drive and steal cars in order to cause as much mayhem as possible, knowing that under tens couldn't be prosecuted. I often wonder if the boy became a school teacher as he was obviously extremely good at teaching!

These offences carried on for several months, succeeding to the point that distraught and aggrieved car owners vented their opinions: 'What are you doing about it?' meaning us. 'How much longer are we to put up with it?' 'What do we pay your wages for?' etc., at many police stations in the area until, one day, I saw this fifteen-year-old driving a stolen Mark 2 Cortina.

The call had come out solely as a lost or stolen Cortina that we should keep our eyes peeled for. I was doing my usual perusing of the periphery when there, waiting to come out of a junction I was about to turn into, was the Cortina, and driving it just happened to be the young gentleman in question!

The chase was on! Actually, we were told in driving school that we never chased anyone, only pursued them. Hence my 'pursuance' was on.

I was about to do a hand break turn, as seen on many James Bond movies, until I thought better of it (actually, I had no idea how to do one!) but the adrenalin was pumping high, and a very rapid three-point turn ensued.

By the time I had got there, he was still sitting at the junction waiting for a gap in the traffic!

A little disappointed that there was not going to be any high-speed chase—sorry high-speed pursuance—I pulled alongside him and indicated for him to pull over. He calmly did so.

As I pulled in behind him, he climbed out of the car and politely asked, 'What d'ya want, pig?'

These were the times I had been extensively trained for! One of the very first things I had had to learn 'parrot fashion' in training school was most of the first paragraph of *General Orders*, (a six-inch thick book of everything we would ever need to know about everything that was ever to confront us in the big wide world—almost!) which read, and even today I can still recite: 'Idle and silly remarks are unworthy of notice and should be disregarded!'

Wise, oh so wise!

I didn't actually say, 'Hello, sir. Pleasant day for driving stolen vehicles!' . . . or anything remotely similar . . . But he was correctly cautioned and arrested, and we can leave it at that.

At the police station he was charged and, as you can imagine, much euphoria was experienced at the arrest. At last we'd brought his reign of terror to an end! Car owners all over South London could once again sleep soundly in their beds knowing that such a heinous character had been removed from the street. MBE here we come . . . Well something like that. It was a pleasing arrest though.

He was only charged with three offences—TDA (taking and driving away, as it was then), no insurance, and driving whilst disqualified by reason of age.

The day dawned for his court appearance, and I was fully prepared for a not guilty plea, thereby having to give the full facts as would be required for a not guilty plea. Certain that he was to be locked away and the key destroyed.

Imagine my surprise to find the scruffy, long-haired, baseball-capped, jean-clad, Doc Martin-booted youth I knew, standing in the dock, hair beautifully groomed and washed and wearing a suit! Butter wouldn't have melted in his mouth!

Further to my surprise—he pleaded guilty. This meant that only the brief facts would be given. No previous convictions, etc. No extraneous facts. Nothing but basics!

Possibly everyone in the court was aware of who this youth was and what he had been up to, including the clerk, but apparently excluding the three JPs.

I can remember the central figure of these JPs, after I'd given the basic facts, looking over her half glasses and asking, 'How much pocket money do you get a week, young man?'

'Sixpence, Ma'am,' came the polite reply! It was quite a while ago, but even then 6d wasn't much (2½ pence today!).

'In which case I am going to fine you two pence for stealing the car, two pence for under age driving, and one pence for no insurance. That leaves you with a penny for the rest of the week. Let that be a lesson to you!'

Silent aghastness filled the courtroom, as my 'young teacher' left the dock with a rather supercilious smirk on his face!

Even the clerk slammed his book shut and stalked from the room, leaving the courtroom staring incredulously at the central lady magistrate who simply stared back wondering what all the commotion was about.

What was it I was saying about the law being an ass?

Actually—I feel I must ask—am I being fair? The heat of that moment for me in court, linked with the murder in a pub story I've already related, together with several others I could have told and haven't, obviously caused me to feel that there is an ass in there somewhere!

But... maybe its not just the law that's always at fault. Of course, the police have got to do it right on the street in the first place, but so must those who wield the law at its next stage; the magistrates and judges. And then those who make the law, the governmental bodies, do not they have answers to give? Even then, can we leave it there? The circle is complete, is it not? You have the law made by governmental bodies. Police activate it. The courts act upon what the police tell them about the offenders and the offence as defined by the law that was made by the government, which the police act upon and . . . Round we go again!

And yet we have the stories I've just related, happening all too frequently. Hence the law is called 'an ass'. So is the government, so are the magistrates, so are the police!

So, is there yet another facet to the equation? (Is this making sense or simply giving you a headache! I sometimes do this to myself when I'm trying to work something out!)

The thing is, we're living in a blame culture, a time when it's always somebody else's fault and never our own! Finger pointing! You just need to watch a game of premiership football to see that in action! Blatant fouls are committed on the pitch with gay abandon and the perpetrators always have that 'butter-wouldn't-melt-in-the-mouth' look and say to the ref., 'Who me!?' Similarly, in life, no one wants to take the blame. No one is prepared to stick their head above the parapet and speak up against injustice or things that everyone can see are just plain wrong in case they get it shot off! Trouble is, so often they do . . . and then they blame someone else . . . which proves my point . . . The result is the same—nothing gets done!

So, who, or what, is the ass? The government says, 'It's down to the courts.' And the courts say, 'The government makes the law,' and they both say, 'The police should do it right in the first place!' I think I'll just leave you to make up your own mind! What do you think?

Chapter Six
Ross

All work places I'm sure, have a joker, and Costner Street Police Station was no exception. Ross. Where do I begin in describing Ross? Totally deranged? Yes. Prize one nut? Definitely. Mentally unstable? Without a doubt. First class mate? Gold plated. Life and soul of every party? Absolutely.

I remember Ross chatting with me during my early days at Costner Street, and the fact that he was going round the world on a shoe string. Seeing what was out there before he got too ensconced in his job, settled down with responsibilities, and too old to enjoy it! He really whet my appetite. I was within a hair's breadth of agreeing but the trouble was, I had joined to be a policeman. I was happy at Costner Street and I'd worked hard to get successfully through the cadet corps and initial training. Did I want to give it all up?

The unperturbed, irrepressible Ross had worked it all out. He'd made enquiries and found others had done it and come straight back into the job without missing a beat. He'd also secured a working job on a cruise ship to America and a job with a wayside food joint just outside the Big Apple for starters. After that it would be just a matter of enjoying the trip 'til the money ran out, and then getting another job for the next stretch. Down through the rest of the USA, into South America, over to Australia, New Zealand, and up through the South Pacific—with its palm trees, golden beaches, and grass skirts! Over into the Far East, Thailand, Burma, India and eventually back up through Europe and home to England. Two years should do it! You can see why I was within a hair's breadth of agreeing, can't you? But . . . I got cold feet.

Off went Ross and two years later, he was not only back at Costner Street Police Station, but on the same shift! Who wanted golden beaches and grass skirts anyway? He'd missed out on two years of shift work, rain, cold and wet. Nothing left to say . . . except he had a few stories to tell!

Ross is still one of the most deranged, gold-plated, nutty mates it has ever been my fortune to have! It was just great to have him back. However, you did have to watch your back when he was on duty!

Like the time several of us were writing up reports; round about 4.00 am. Middle of the night. A nightmare time for shift workers, when the only sensible people moving around are cleaners!

The window slowly opened and before anyone knew what was afoot—in floated a hat stand, complete with hats, landing in the middle of the table and sending books, papers, pens, cups of tea, sandwiches, and not least, personnel, all over the room. A head followed, looking like the cat that got the cream, mouthing something like, 'I thought you'd all dropped off!' The weird thing was, we accepted it! It was just Ross!

P.S. If anyone had dropped off—they were now awake!

I was riding shotgun in a panda one day (that means I was the radio operator—not a gun in sight in those days. No gun toting. Truncheon only.) with Ross driving. It was a beautiful sunny Sunday afternoon. Birds were singing. The smell of freshly mown grass was wafting in on a warm breeze through the open car windows. Mums, dads, and offspring were all out enjoying themselves with grandma and granddad sleeping in deckchairs. Checked table cloths laden with cucumber and tomato sandwiches adorned the greenery of the parks, as did bikini-clad ladies! Not that we noticed the bikinis, of course. We were out 'by-the-book' policing in order that our public were able to enjoy such pastimes. Minds fully on the job and all that. It would have to be more than a checked table cloth to take our minds off the job in hand!

As per usual with Ross, it was a fun-filled, laugh a minute late turn tour. As we left the park and were wending our way back to the station for a cuppa, Ross stopped at a set of traffic lights. We were in the nearside lane and, as we waited, a small green car, containing two elderly ladies pulled up beside us. Nothing strange in that, which left me somewhat befused (confused and befuddled mixed) to see the looks of utter 'befusement' on the ladies' faces as we pulled away!

They didn't move, car and occupants sitting rigid at the lights! I was about to ask what had caused their consternation, when, as he turned towards me, he wiggled a bright red, five-inch tongue from between his teeth! I would have loved to have been a fly on the wall of the old ladies' car. I can only imagine the comments in their vehicle as an employee of the Crown waved a cheery 'Hello' with a five-inch tongue!

I suppose my most vivid memory of Ross was the lemon squeezy incident! Do you remember the plastic lemon, full of lemon juice? Once empty and refilled with water, they made an excellent water pistol—to Ross's delight! He was a dab hand with it. An artist. You could swear he had nothing in his hand and yet you'd catch a squirt in the eye with gay abandon. Writing reports. Having deep meaningful conversations. Even talking to members of the public! I can even remember on one occasion, whilst on parade, the superintendent walked in for one of his infrequent 'quality checks'—uniform pressed, shoes clean, hair smart, pocket book, whistle, truncheon, etc., etc.

He was just about to give an encouraging pep talk when I saw a thin jet of water slicing through the air and catching him just above the left eye! He looked up and searched the ceiling for tell tail evidence of water! To this day he thought we had a leak in the station!

He was the gaffer, incidentally, who was on the sharp end of an old trick—raise the toilet seat, stretch cling-film over the aperture, and replace the seat! Who did it and what the outcome was, no one ever found out. One can only speculate!

It was another warm Sunday afternoon and East Street market was in full swing and knee deep in people. For us this meant pick pockets, unlicensed street traders, three card sharps, lost purses, and lost children. And daft questions like, 'Could you tell me where Bucking Abbey is, please?' or 'Aren't you hot in all that gear?' In short, it meant mountains of work!

I tried to stay out of the market as much as possible, and thus I was wandering up and down the main street, still chock-a-block with people, but at least not quite on each other's heels, when Ross pulled up in our plain and unmarked CID car.

He was in the passenger seat and urgently flagged me to the car window. Believing something was going down, I hot footed it to the vehicle. Maybe the heat or the volume of people had got to me, I'm not sure, but my brain was quite obviously in neutral until it was too late, and the ubiquitous lemon squeezer came into view.

I jumped to avoid the well-directed jet, but too late, and was caught fully in my unblinking left eye.

As soon as the deed was done, the CID car roared off into the distance, leaving me floundering. I'm not quite sure, floundering is the right word because as I jumped backwards, my right heel caught on the pavement edge, causing me to loose balance and sprawl extremely ungainly backwards across the pavement, narrowly missing pedestrians, who in their turn were trying to avoid this somersaulting policeman! My helmet went one way, I went the other, finishing up almost through a shop window, very much on my backside! Slowly rising and trying to avoid the onlooking stares, I collected my helmet and, head down, started to wander off pretending nothing had happened.

Seconds later, I was aware of a very aged lady tottering across the road. She was ignoring the horns of the cars and trying desperately to attract my attention. As I turned to her, she waved a piece of paper at me shouting, 'It's okay, Officer. I've got his number. I've got his number!'

Apart from all the crackpot stuff that went with Ross, he was also very helpful, like the time we were on patrol together and he bought a plant pot. He promptly stuck it inside his helmet, to the obvious amusement of the shop keeper, replaced same and we wandered out of the shop. Common sense really, isn't it? If you think about it, where, in a tight-fitting uniform, could you carry a plant pot? Many of us took tips from this, and on several occasions, were able to get fish and chips back to the station unnoticed! We didn't go courting until we'd had a shower, of course, but we had had a substantial meal in the mean time!

There was one time where Ross actually got his! Not in the way any of us, or him, thought he would. Well, he didn't get his—he got hers! You'll see what I mean in a minute.

Ross had a bit of an old banger (didn't we all in those days!) for getting backwards and forwards to work and on one occasion the exhaust came loose. It hadn't fallen off nor did it sound like an elephant with a cold; it just rattled a bit.

So, when his break was due, he decided to try and tighten it up before anything worse happened. In those days, we had to park in nearby streets as the police yard had no room to park a roller skate, let alone a car!

We had to be a little circumspect in the where and how and when we parked . . . They did belong to policemen after all, and I knew a lot of people in that area, at that time, who would have loved to know which car was whose—for obvious reasons. We actually had surprisingly little trouble in the couple of years I worked there.

Back to the story. Ross had been tinkering for only a few minutes when he became aware of someone approaching. At first, being under the car, he couldn't see who it was, but he wasn't in the least bit worried because he was having a serious problem with one of the nuts. He'd skinned his knuckles and had rust in his eye, and worst of all, had run out of the expletives which were keeping him somewhat sane!

At that point, the footsteps stopped. Although his head and shoulders were under the vehicle, he could still see the legs and feet stationary beside him—and what a vision of loveliness it was! Normally Ross enjoyed the sight of a well-turned ankle and particularly when encased in stockings rather than tights, but on this occasion, he knew the owner. One stocking was round her ankle, while the other was at half-mast. To say the legs were slender would be an insult to slender people—a chicken would have had more meat on them! The ensemble was completed by a pair of Doc Martins; old, uncleaned and with an aroma of well-matured Gorgonzola.

Ross had arrested this particular lady on many occasions for multifarious offences; from every kind of alcohol abuse imaginable, through soliciting to violence, shoplifting and beyond. Now I'm not saying that the lady recognised Ross from the lower torso protruding from under the car, but at that moment, she casually opened her legs and watered the footpath. Literally weed and walked on! The fact that most of it missed the footpath and hit Ross's legs was beside the point or maybe *was* the point!

I never did ask Ross if he got that nut loose.

Chapter Seven
Demonstrations: The Marches Begin

It was the late sixties and the 'Anti Whatever-cum-Everything Marches' were about to descend upon us.

There were lots of issues burning worldwide at that time that were causing certain factions of society to stretch 'Freedom of Speech' to its limit—regrettably nothing changes . . .

I'm all for freedom of speech for the person who has a genuine gripe and needs to be able to have his say—after all, ideas, inventions, good changes, etc., come from those who have stuck their head above the parapet and said, 'Maybe there is a better way,' or 'Is the law correct here?' or 'Man's inhumanity to man is extremely prevalent in this situation. What can we do about it?' My problem is with those that have selfish motives who use free speech for their own ends or simply to 'trouble make!'

Wikipedia says: 'Freedom of speech is a principle that supports the freedom of an individual or a community to articulate their opinions and ideas without fear of retaliation, censorship or legal sanction.' The European Convention of Human Rights, Article 10 says: 'Everyone has the right to freedom of expression. This right shall include freedom to hold opinions, or to receive and impart information and ideas without interference by a public authority and regardless of frontiers.' It goes on to explain that this right comes with responsibilities.

So, does this all mean that everybody has the right to say whatever they like, about whatever they like, whenever they like! I sincerely hope not. I'm just delighted that there are men and women with much greater intellect than me who are being paid to discuss such matters in order that we can live in a free society. An unenviable task, being made even harder by those I mentioned before, who 'want to stretch these boundaries to their limit'.

However, as far as I was concerned in those days, demonstrations meant overtime. Mercenary, I know, but my job was to uphold the law (and do as I was told) so, if I was told to go to a demonstration and prevent any breaches of the peace, then to a demonstration I would go. The fact that I may have had a weekly leave cancelled—with less than eight days' notice, therefore double time and another weekly leave given in lieu—had nothing to do with it. That wasn't mercenary was it . . . ? I was simply doing as I was told! Wasn't I?

* * *

It was a Saturday afternoon and I had been patrolling for around seven hours, only an hour to the 'off', and I was thinking about what I was going to do that night—I had nothing arranged, but I knew of a nurse's party on in Wandsworth—when the radio barked at me 'Serious disturbance in Grosvenor Square outside the American Embassy. Officers required.' I wasn't far from the nick and made my way in to find out what was going on.

It turned out that some students were demonstrating about the war in Vietnam outside the embassy and the local police station were wanting assistance to help contain it. Nothing much more than that, but if I wanted to go, it would be continuous duty and classed as overtime.

Party or money? No contest and so half a dozen of us waited to be transported up to the scene. After an hour of waiting, the message came through that containment had been achieved and we weren't needed. Overtime of one hour meant money *and* party. Perfect.

On arrival at the station the following day, it transpired that the demonstration of the previous day had blown-up again in the night and a group of us were to go up and await further direction.

The van transported us to the area where we were then transferred to a 'Green Goddess'—an ancient single decker green bus. I'm not saying it was old, but I could swear it had solid rubber tyres! The seats were torn and had only enough knee room for a twelve-year-old. Two twelve-year-olds sitting side by side would have just about fitted on those seats, possibly, but not two six-foot-plus, fifteen-stone-plus policemen. Rather tight, as you can imagine. There had been a strong smell of leather, dust, decay, and damp when we climbed on board, which rapidly disappeared as a full contingent of personnel got themselves entrenched!

We didn't realise it at the time, but this was to be our home for the next twelve hours—with only a stale cheese sandwich and a biscuit for dinner. We didn't even get tea on that occasion. Very different, so I'm told, for the lads today. Thank goodness.

We were stationed round some forgotten corner, near enough to the action if we were needed, but otherwise forgotten.

After an hour or so someone found a couple of packs of cards, which kept some of us happy for a while; then the snoring started; then the, 'What's going on, Sarge?' Replied with, 'We're trying to find out.' It was obvious that information was getting lost, but as eight hours approached, we became more upbeat as we realised that a bit more cash was going to be forthcoming. Overtime! At twelve hours, the message came, 'Stand down.'

Stand down! We'd never stood up, and now it was almost impossible to stand up, down, or any other position. We were seized to the seats. The aroma that must have been issuing from the bus can only be imagined as twenty hairy coppers emerged back into the sunlight.

'Not needed,' was to become quite common over the next weeks. We were simply 'Standby, in case needed.' Credit must be due to someone as conditions slowly improved—wish I knew who the someone was! Several of us would certainly buy him or her a drink. At least by then we managed to get a decent sandwich, even a slice of cake and a cup of tea several times during the twelve-hour stints.

More packs of cards, chess sets, etc. were brought in to alleviate the boredom of non-action until one shift. 'Form up'. We'd only been there an hour or so. 'Look lively, lads. It's gone tits up!'

That turned out to be an understatement. Bear in mind none of us had had any training for these situations. It was new to everyone. The only thing I was to learn at a later date was 'the trudge', whereby a single line of policemen, the only line of defence between the mob and where we weren't going to allow them to go, linked arms and on the command word 'trudge' stepped forward with the right foot and literally v-trudged into the mob, specifically to split them into two groups. I know it sounds very Heath Robinson, but amazingly, it worked to perfection. At a later demonstration, it was to save me from an extremely difficult and dangerous situation. (Oh, and the other thing we were later taught was that should someone throw 'a noxious substance' in our faces we were to urinate in our hands and wash our eyes out with it!) That was the extent of the teaching received in those days

I'm getting ahead of myself, none of this training had been given at this stage, we were simply the 'thin blue line', and I mean thin. One, maybe two lines of policemen to block off an entire road to several thousand demonstrators. Crazy, but to a degree, in those days at least, it worked.

As we climbed from the coach, every emotion possible hit us; fear to excitement; blasé comments to silence; looks of bravado to wobbly knees. What were we about to face? How dodgy was the situation? I could only imagine how those amazing blokes back in war days felt as they ran from the landing crafts onto the beaches of Dunkirk. For us, in a sense, it was action at last, but at least we weren't going to face guns, mortars and tanks—were we?

As we got to the scene, we were formed up into the two obligatory lines across a junction, with approximately twenty men in each row, and around five to six thousand demonstrators in front of us. Quite an awe-inspiring sight. King Canute had nothing on what we faced.

I stood for a few minutes trying to come to grips with what was happening in front of us when, suddenly, I became aware of movement behind me. A huge presence appeared by my right shoulder.

Mounted policemen on horseback. It's difficult to explain the feeling of almost euphoria that came over the atmosphere as these incredible animals sidled their warm bodies in beside and around us. Anyone who has ever seen them in central London or at events will know how wonderful they are in crowd control scenarios. Huge, awe-inspiring, trained to perfection and fantastic to have on your side!

For a while there was quite a friendly banter taking place around my position between 'us and them', until the face of the inspector on the horse beside me seemed to explode! It took a while for me, or anyone else, to realise what had happened, but it turned out a 'demonstrator' had thrown a sharpened penny (that's an old penny, approximately an inch or 2½ cm in diameter, with its edges honed to razor sharpness) at him, skimming fashion, the edge of which had caught him on the cheek, splitting his face from mouth to ear.

Panic broke out among the demonstrators (at least the ones with honest intent) as they realised, 'We didn't sign up for this!' and that one of their number was a 'rogue'. Someone who was not there for the cause but was simply there to make trouble.

Regrettably, there are always those who seek out this sort of occasions to glory in mischief. It never matters where, football matches, demonstrations, anywhere where numerous people are gathered together, somewhere where they can cowardly appear incognito. Here was such a person (and such an event) and as so often happens, one that melted back into the crowd, never to be seen again once the act was perpetrated.

The snag was, on this occasion, there was more than one; the sharpened penny was immediately followed by a tin of red paint further up the line. Horses, policemen, and demonstrators alike, covered in red paint. It was pure carnage. How no one else was hurt I'll never know, but the demonstration broke up extremely rapidly. This was not what anyone had joined up for.

The demonstrations slowly became more and more fragile as people with all types of grievances vented their feelings on society. Regrettably, it also opened the door for the trouble makers. One could almost feel them rubbing their hands with glee as they invented more ways to upset the status quo.

On one specific demonstration I met such a person. I won't mention what the demonstration was about as the last thing I would want to do is to paint everyone there with the same brush. Safe to say that this cause did lend itself to such people being in attendance.

I found myself once again on the front row, arms tightly linked with an unknown colleague, facing some umpteen thousand demonstrators all chanting the tune for the day. The press was such that even with horses behind us, it was difficult to keep position.

One particular chanter, more vociferous than the others, realised that pushing in a particular way could have serious consequences on the 'thin blue line'. The act was extremely dangerous, as one false move and the entire section would collapse and we'd be trampled under pure weight of numbers. Police and demonstrator alike! He had no thought for such an outcome and continued to disrupt.

I happened to catch his eye on one occasion, and with a definite glint therein, he pushed his particular push again, as if to say, 'Catch me if you can!' At that specific moment he knew that I knew that he knew that I could do nothing about it as he was two to three rows back. Gay abandonment continued.

However, the pressure behind him was such that there were occasions when he was forced closer to the front than he would have liked. I watched and bided my time.

Then on one specific surge from his colleagues, he was forced into grabbing distance. I didn't hesitate, and clung on for grim death, attempting to pull him into arresting distance.

He was quite strong, probably due to pure fear and adrenalin. Being so intent on arresting him, I didn't realise this until it was too late, I had been pulled onto his turf rather than my pulling him onto mine! I was some six to seven rows inside their group with his specific mates around me chanting my collar number and 'You're dead. You're dead,' in my ear.

Not the most pleasant of circumstances to find oneself in! All I could think was, 'Pudding. You've done it now!' or words to that effect—when I suddenly became aware that the throng around me had changed clothing! No longer did I have civilian-garbed persons around me but men in blue! Numbers on their collars and everything.

The amazing, incredible, indefatigable 'trudge' had done its work. A wedge had been pushed in towards me, opened at its point, popping me through and then closing and merging back into our lines. Many things were to be said about the trudge in the days that followed, but believe me . . . mine were *all* positive.

Things are very different today with shields, helmets, new

tactics, etc., etc., in use and the 'trudge', I believe, long forgotten. But, for me . . . Long live the trudge!

* * *

I've always been a clean living, honest sort of guy. Too chicken to have been a villain of any description. I like to go to bed with a clean conscience—I find it much easier to sleep that way.

On top of that, I have never sworn in my life! Not even the slightest word has slipped out of my mouth. Even in the tensest of situations! Mind you, I do 'flip' a lot. You know 'flipping this' and 'flipping that' (well—there must be a release of tension of some sort, eh?)—but when my mates would say to me, 'Have a good " ✗ ✱ ✦ ☂ !" and be done with it!' I would reply 'I could "flip" in front of the Queen and I doubt she'd be offended . . . Could you give your retort?'

You're probably sitting with your finger half way down your throat, thinking, 'What sort of guy is this?' Bear with me and please don't put my book away . . . I'm certainly not perfect and I doubt that perfect people exist anyway.

But one early turn Sunday morning, what could have been a dodgy situation became interesting, to say the least, and that was because of my 'peculiar-to-some' habit of not swearing.

It was a beautiful day. Busy, but beautiful. The only down side was that I was posted to street market duty! Three card merchants. Unlicensed street traders. Pick pockets. Lost property, including children—you know the sort of thing. People, people, and more people.

But when the sun is shining and everybody is out to enjoy themselves, laughing, cheery chat, everything feels good, the atmosphere is great, and you can't help but feel on top of the world.

Nothing was going to upset me, not even the bloke with a monkey. Yes, a monkey.

He was using it as a photo aid. Sitting it in mum's hand bag or on little Johnny's head then taking a quick photo and charging a fiver for the privilege! Promising to forward the finished product on ASAP.

In one sense (providing he did 'send it on ASAP') quite the entrepreneur, in another, illegal! You need a licence.

You might think, 'Well it was a nice thing to do! Nice memories for the future.' I agree, but what about all the other street venders who had bought licences and were paying for their pitches? They weren't too happy with him, or me if I ignored it. If you want to sell, you needed a licence.

But I was in a good mood. Nothing was going to upset it and I thought 'a verbal warning will suffice.'

The only snag was, as I went round the corner, out he came again. We met up some twenty minutes later.

'That's taking the mick, mate! When I say pack up and go home, I mean it! If you want to trade, get a licence!'

Cap in hand and bowed head, he said, 'I'm sorry, guv. Only trying to make a living.'

I was still in a good mood and thought, 'Well, live and let live,' and gave him a second verbal warning.

A little later, and for the third time, I again caught him sticking his monkey in a lady's handbag! Enough was enough and in the book he went.

Later that day, as I returned to the nick, I was met by the station sergeant. 'Hi John. Have a run in with the monkey man today?'

I was whistling, 'She'll be coming round the mountain when she comes' or some such tune as I was still in a good mood. I was somewhat taken aback. 'Run in?' I said.

'Yep. Came in and told me he didn't mind being reported but when you pumped a few 'Fs' into him he didn't like it!'

My good mood was rapidly slipping round the U-bend. I'd let him off twice before reporting him!

'Serge, I have never sworn in my life and, yes, I reported him but . . .'

Before I could say another word, the sergeant raised his hand to stop me and said, 'I looked monkey man straight in the eye and said, any other officer at this station and I may have believed you. But this one? I could probably get every member of his shift to make a statement saying they'd never heard him swear in his life.' Apparently the colour had started to drain from his face, either because he'd been caught out or because he was getting frog marched out of the station.

Chapter Eight
Do You Know Who's in the Other Car?

Is it possible that those of us who have been driving for a long time become, dare I say, blasé about driving? Do we ever think, 'It'll never happen to us!' as we drive just that little bit too fast in the fog, or when we're trying to get to an appointment on time, or as we look at a car in a ditch on a frosty morning, or someone that had touched their brakes and slithered into the car in front?

More to the point, although our car is regularly serviced and in a good condition, is the one in front or behind us? And just because we're in good health, with double 'A' vision and sharp reflexes, it doesn't mean that everyone on the road is in such a state.

I remember driving the 6.00 am to 2.00 pm early shift in a panda one February morning. There had been a heavy frost when I left for work at 5.00 am but it had apparently disappeared by the time I got in my panda at Costner Street. I did say *apparently*.

While still thinking to myself, 'These roads look okay, but I'm certainly not taking any chances!' I became aware of a Ford Anglia in front of me, not speeding, but taking corners a little too fast for my liking in those conditions.

I was thinking of stopping him over the next junction and giving him a gentle warning about having more thought for the road service when I saw the traffic light turn from green to amber.

I intended to draw alongside him and signal him to pull in when, to my horror, he made no attempt to stop or slow down at the red light, but continued straight over the junction! He didn't speed up, slow down, or make any attempt to stop. Simply carried on as if he hadn't seen them. I caught up with him a little farther down the road, and after several attempts, managed to get him to see me and pull in.

As he got out from his car, he approached me, and with a very well manufactured accent said, 'Hello, Officer, and what can I do for you?'

I must admit his politeness took me back a little. I was still thinking about the 10–15 yards of red light he had just crossed, and how fortunate he had been that nothing had been coming the other way. The warning for the icy conditions was a distant memory.

I cautioned him, explained what I had seen, to which he replied 'Unfortunately, Officer, you are incorrect. Those lights were not red, they were definitely blue.'

How does one respond to that? I had correctly cautioned him and therefore all words spoken after such, are taken down verbatim and used as evidence. When the case got to court, he did receive a somewhat old-fashioned look from the magistrate. I never did find out the actual condition of his eyes . . . but not so with a similar incident sometime later, when another gentleman failed to stop at a red light.

Again, I was able to stop the vehicle without much trouble, and as the driver climbed from the car, I could see he was around retirement age, with a good build and wearing a suit. However, his most distinguishing features were not his cloths, age, or build, but the bottle-bottom spectacles he wore!

I realised the poor chap couldn't help his eyesight, but those specks frightened me to death! They reminded me of an old *Peanuts* sketch where a couple of crabs living at the bottom of a rock pool would occasionally look up and see eyeballs looking back at them (it was actually a dog gazing into the water) but they would shiver with fright whimpering, 'Eyeballs in the sky! Eyeballs in the sky!' The glasses magnified his eyes to such an extent that all else was obliterated! No head, just eyes! I didn't even see his mouth move as he said, 'Yes, Officer. Can I help you?'

I answered rather fumblingly and hoped he didn't think I was being facetious when I said, 'Did you not see the traffic lights?'

He answered as I should have expected, 'What traffic lights?'

I turned and pointed to the lights now some 50 yards away. 'Those ones.' I saw him squint as he stared up the street.

'Of course,' came the reply.

Now whether he saw the lights or not was not my immediate concern, the condition of his eyesight *was*, and as a police officer, I had the power to request a simple eyesight test there and then. Which I did!

I explained to him what was going to happen, to which he became extremely agitated . . . objectionable was probably a better word! Objection after objection, in fact!

Eventually I said, 'Look, if you can pass my very simple test here and now, there's no problem and you can be on your way. If you refuse to take it, then I'll have to ask you to come to the police station where a proper test will be arranged, and that will be time consuming for us both.'

'Okay,' he said begrudgingly, 'I've nothing to hide. What do I have to do?'

'Simple,' I replied. 'Just read me a car number from 20 yards away.'

I looked around and approximately 20 yards down the road and parked on the same side of the road as ourselves, was a VW Beetle with its square rear number plate facing towards us. I pointed to the car and waited.

He stared down the road for a while and then said, 'Which car?'

I said, 'That one. The Beetle.' And again, pointed to it.

He was obviously having trouble and I said, 'Just walk towards that parked car down there and as soon as you can read its number, tell me what it is.'

He started towards it. Twenty yards, 19, 18 ... 10, 9, 8 ... I was having trouble believing what was happening, but eventually, at ten feet from the car, he bent down and gave me the correct number!

Obtaining his keys and explaining the best course of action for him and other road users was for him to have an immediate eyesight test. It took some time—the details of which I won't bore you with now—to explain he could have them back when he had obtained a document from an optician which said he was okay to drive.

So adamant was he that he didn't need an eyesight test that—as I found out later at court—he never got one. At court, he continued to argue with the judge, even after he was disqualified until he got the test. Did he ever get a test ... not a clue!

As I said earlier, you can be the greatest driver in the world, in tip-top physical condition and have a perfectly well-maintained vehicle, but you just never know who's in the car in front of you. Or behind you! You just need to know that that bloke is going to stop when you do—don't you?

Talking about well-maintained cars and yet another set of traffic lights ... I'd been driving behind a Ford Thames van for quite some time. He hadn't really caused me to take much notice of him—until he went straight through a red light at a particularly busy junction. Fortunately, there hadn't been any 'amber-gamblers' in the other road.

Eventually I stopped him and approached the vehicle. A very pleasant young chap said, 'I know. I know. It was the red light, wasn't it? I tried to stop but my handbrake wouldn't work.'

I said, 'Your handbrake wouldn't work? Why didn't you use the foot break?'

To which he turned and retrieved his brake master cylinder from the back seat! 'It's knackered. That's where I'm going now. To get it fixed.'

Feeling—and probably looking—somewhat like a rabbit caught in headlights, I said, 'And this is yours?' indicating his master cylinder, 'From this vehicle?'

He nodded.

Upon further examination, I found his footbrake went straight to the floor without any resistance whatsoever (not that I was expecting any as it should have been connected to the master cylinder which he had in his hand!) and that under the bonnet, the push rod was flapping about through the bulk head! For those of us who are not mechanically minded, the master cylinder is the bit under the bonnet that connects the footbrake to the rest of the breaking system, enabling the car to stop. That's what was on the back seat!

It was another vehicle for traffic division to examine.

Remember. They're about!

They were 'about' in other places too, not necessarily just on the road. I remember a discussion taking place on the radio between a couple of colleagues and the control room about an incident to which they had been called, a few streets away from where I was patrolling.

Apparently, a lady had been heard continuously screaming in a block of flats off Comer Road. A single scream could mean anything. Several screams set your heart pounding and your feet running as, invariably, someone is in dire need of help. Continuous screaming, again, could mean anything from someone desperately needing help, to someone with their finger stuck in the door, to someone deliberately scratching their nails down a blackboard for devilment.

Whatever the reason, screaming can't be ignored!

On this occasion, the first officer on the scene had arrived to find a bevy of neighbours all looking up at a second floor flat from where the tumult was coming.

'She's been doing it all morning!' one had said.

'Started before I was out of bed,' said another.

'Olive, next door to her, gets it all the time.'

'Sings to her own tune, that one.'

'Daft as a barrel of monkeys.'

On and on went the comments.

Tony, the PC first on scene, had gleaned quite a bit of information, like name and address, but most importantly, 'I wouldn't go in her house if you paid me!' had been commented by a resident.

'Why's that?' Tony had asked

'If you don't go in with someone else, she'll eat you alive!'

The terminology had set him, as one of Costner Streets finest officers, thinking, 'I wonder why not?'

Sensibly, he'd called for backup just in case!

That hadn't done much good as both him and Sid had attempted to approach the flat without success. They'd simply been met by a verbal barrage—and a brush handle! I think the brush handle had been the decider for more backup to be called for.

It probably wasn't just the brush handle, but the apparition that was holding it that had made up their minds. A lady somewhere between thirty and forty, slim build (once-upon-a-time quite pretty as we were later to find out) but at the time, a snarling rictus embodied the face, teeth bared, drool from the corner of her mouth, both corners in fact, including the middle, a deep red to purple in colour (her face, not the drool), hair untouched by a comb that week—correction, if ever! Putting everything together, a rather sorry picture.

It was obvious that the situation was beyond police intervention and that specialist help was needed.

By the time I arrived, the poor lady was crying more than screaming. She didn't appear to be English, in that whatever she was shouting made no sense. One word in particular was being repeated over and over, 'Wilayhee'. Nobody knew what it meant at the time, but I've never forgotten it or ever been able to get it translated.

There was something in her tone that really pulled at my heart strings and before I knew what I was doing, I found myself on the second-floor balcony and approaching the distraught woman. I knew a doctor was en route and thought, 'What in the world am I doing up here? Leave it to the professionals!' How would I succeed where the others had failed!

It was a weird, surreal situation, and as I approached her, she started to raise her brush handle. Suddenly I was aware of speaking very calmly to her. I haven't a clue what I said, but realising I should have been watching the broom, I found myself listening to myself!

Slowly she lowered her brush and just stared at me, repeating 'Wilayhee.' An amazing transformation came over her and instead of the maniacal, sobbing screamer, she dropped to her knees and clutched my legs, and started whispering, 'Wilayhee'—you can see why I never forgot the word—and instead of being vicious and unapproachable, she became quite the opposite. Very much the opposite. She became amorous ... extremely amorous! I continued to talk calmly, feeling anything but calm and realised I was now the one who needed help—for different reasons! Instead of listening to myself I started thinking, 'How do I get out of this?'

It was at that point that two gents in white coats arrived and took over the calm chat. They were amazing, gentle, kind, understanding. I've never been so grateful to see anybody in my life.

I never found out what had been going on in her head, but really hope she found the peace she was so desperately in need of as they each took a hand and slowly lifted her to her feet. She continued to whisper 'Wilayhee' as they wandered off to the waiting ambulance.

I've often thought since, 'Why did I behave like that? A strange reality to be faced with. What made me do it?' I assure you, I'm no hero and am quite aware of my failings, but something very real took hold. Here was an obviously mentally unstable lady, but also a very unhappy one. I suppose it's a bit like a baby's crying is intended to tug at mum's heartstrings. Well maybe something like that was happening inside me and I heard a cry for help in this situation. It would have been much easier to have simply stood with my mates and waited for the professionals, but the easy way out isn't always best. Just easier!

Who knows why this woman was as she was? Had she been like it from birth? Was there a biological malfunction somewhere in her wiring? Had something unenviable happened at some point in her life?

I remember once arresting a drunk for being 'drunk and incapable'. i.e. flat out on the pavement. As I waited for the van to come and collect us, I can still see that totally undesirable figure stretched out before me. Dirty, smelly, helpless. Did I see something crawling from his hair down the back of his neck? I didn't investigate. Just waited and continued to make sure he was still breathing (when I'd taken a deep enough breath to get close enough to check, without having to breath in and allow that horrendously obnoxious gas being emitted from his mouth to enter my lungs!).

As a young sprog, these were the types of arrest on which we cut our baby teeth. These were the ways we learnt the basic procedure from arrest through to paperwork, charging, and finally court.

It never ceased to amaze me how different things were with your prisoner the following morning when you could sit and chat lucidly together before your case was heard. Sometimes you heard how everybody was wrong and that it was completely the world's fault that they were in this situation. Wives, jobs, bosses. Their stories were hugely multifarious. But the story of this dirty, smelly, lice-ridden, old drunk never left me.

He had been a doctor. Married with three young children. A boy of twelve, and two girls, one eight and the other five. They'd been returning from holidays in their family Rover when he had turned to admonish one of the girls in the back seat. His wife had screamed and as he turned back to look out of the windscreen, he had been confronted with a tractor emerging from a field. He hadn't had time to break or swerve and had hit the vehicle full on the side, killing his wife, three children and the farmer almost instantly.

Only he had survived.

As I looked at him that morning, he began weeping and saying, 'Why me? Why me? Why should I be alive?'

What a paradigm shift! One minute a dirty, old vagrant, the next a tragic doctor who was unable to forgive himself for something that was probably not his fault in the first place. You never know who you're talking to!

Who was the 'Wilayhee' woman, really?

Many was the time my 'gut' was to speak to me over the next thirty years, from 'Stop that car!' to 'Deal gently' with this one. I can honestly say that I don't think my 'gut' ever let me down!

I suppose when you join one of the 'caring professions'—NHS, fire brigade, police—you do it as a calling. It's certainly not for the money. You just want, or hope, to be able to help someone, somehow, albeit probably just in small ways.

A bit like the little boy walking along a starfish strewn beach . . . The tide, as it ebbed, had left hundreds, if not thousands, of starfish marooned and destined to a hot, dry, sun-roasted existence and eventual death.

Unable to help themselves, the little boy was picking them up, one at a time, and throwing them back into the sea.

A man walking the opposite way approached the boy and said, 'I'm sorry to tell you, but you're completely wasting your time! Look at the thousands of starfish that are left. You're making no difference at all!'

The little boy bent down, picked up another, threw it back into the sea and said, 'Well, maybe I've made a difference to that one.'

Who was it that said, 'You can't help everybody everywhere, but you can help somebody somewhere'?

Chapter Nine
Wheels and More

One of my claims to fame (actually my only claim to fame) was the fact that I was on the first panda course in the Met! It wasn't by choice, just that I had a full driving licence and was in the right place at the right time; therefore, I was put on the course. If I'd been given the choice, I would still have jumped at it. I've always loved driving; loved the freedom it gives, loved the feeling of having those 'horses' under my shoe. Getting from A to B was a lot quicker than on Shanks's pony anyway! Plus, the fact that I'd been an avid watcher of *Z Cars* (showing my age somewhat!) tearing around the streets with a blue light flashing. What wasn't there to like? Especially for a young nineteen-year-old! I wouldn't even have to pay for the petrol—or the driving course! Mind you, doing it right and doing it like the screen stars, are two different things.

Obviously everything we were taught had a reason. One statement I will always remember my driving instructor giving was: 'Any fool can drive fast enough to be dangerous!'

How true!

Extensive training was therefore required in how to drive fast— in the right places—safely; the importance of 'car sympathy', (e.g. no ratchet-sounding as one pulled on the hand break—coffees all round offence that one); always reversing into parking bays, etc., were some of the things I would learn on the many courses I was to attend at Hendon, the police driving school, as well as the training school, in the years to come on my way to becoming an eventual class one advanced driver. I did say I was a petrol head, didn't I? However, to get to that level took a lot of studying and hard work, but as no doubt every other class one would feel, we're quite proud of the accomplishment.

Everybody must start somewhere, and the panda course was a basic training course of two weeks, giving, on successful completion, a grade five. The subsequent courses to take, depending on what you wished to achieve, would take you through further grades from four to one through van driving to fast response vehicles. In those days this would mean in excess of two months of nine-to-five tuition, but not all at the same time.

On leaving training school as a panda grade five driver, I was to be the first probationer at Costner Street to ever have a driving grade. Much to the chagrin of many longer serving officers.

Understandably so! Some had walked the streets for many years and never been inside a police car. To the credit of those men serving with me at that time, I was always treated with respect. Even though it meant, on occasions, me driving much longer serving men around.

Fortunately, conditions were changing in the police service. Permanently walking the beats for twenty years was becoming a thing of the past and often as young PCs we would get postings to the R/T car—the fast response vehicle of its day.

It was a posting always looked forward to by the young 'uns; big, exciting calls; big arrests; chases (or pursuits as we had to call them—one never chased anybody, only pursued them—let the other vehicle make the mistake); quality class one driving; dry and warm for three weeks. What wasn't there to like?

Each vehicle would have an operator, who operated the radio and sat in the front seat, an observer, who observed anything and everything and sat in the back, and a driver who drove, and sat in the front!

It was imperative that the vehicle was checked over before being taken out as anything from loose wheel nuts to dry radiators, empty petrol tanks, or deflated tyres could have occurred during its previous eight hours. Sometimes without the knowledge of the last driver, sometimes because he was in such a rush that things simply got forgotten.

As the next driver, you had to know that if you were in some high-speed pursuit or attempting to get from A to B in the shortest time, the vehicle was not going to let you down or suffer some terminal illness to itself or, more importantly, its occupants!

There were other types of circumstances of course: from out of nowhere would step a wall, or a gap would suddenly shrink before the driver could negotiate it . . . quite amazing what inanimate objects could get up to. The result would be hours of paperwork for the unfortunate police driver who fell foul of these hidden 'nasties'!

Hence, the next shift driver had to do thorough checks.

Early turn was just about to begin and, as such, a check was being undertaken by the driver. Ron, the observer for the tour, rested his hand on the front nearside wing to watch the proceedings. He felt a slight greasiness to the wing surface and as he took his hand away, found it covered in black paint. Upon further examination he found that the entire wing had undergone a respray!

At that precise moment, the night duty driver ran out, 'Watch the wing, we had an upsy-daisy last night—'

Seeing his warning had come too late, he related his story.

The night had just begun with the ubiquitous street crawl, that period when nothing was happening, nothing was moving, everything was still, and you're crawling around looking for something, anything to occur to relieve the boredom of the moment, when suddenly, an unseen dustbin jumped from the kerb (noticing the driver looking the other way of course) right into the path of the front nearside wing!

The cat sitting on the dustbin lid had been the hidden catalyst for the entire crew's heart attack as its death-curdling scream of fright had reverberated around the entire forsaken street.

Cedric slammed on his anchors, jumped out, and examined the wing. Slight dent. Slight scratches. Just enough to earn him three weeks writing and relief from driving for six months!

He got on his hands and knees to examine the offended part more closely. Gently rubbing it, dare I say caressing it, so that, as if by magic, he could make it disappear. Slowly rising, shaking his head, he uttered the driver's lament, those never to be forgotten words, 'Bollocks!'

Nothing had been happening. Nothing was happening and so Cedric made the decision—'I've got a panel beating mate not far from here . . .'

I didn't know whether this had been quick thinking, idiotic thinking, or simply suicidal thinking, but rightly or wrongly, the repair had been carried out, and Ron got a black hand for his trouble! A further quick 'blow-over' by Cedric's mate sorted the problem, and no-one was any the wiser. Apart from us.

It was a little later during that particular early turn tour that the R/T car picked a wet, bedraggled 'me' up.

I hated early turn with a passion. No, more like an utter loathsomeness, and to be wet into the bargain just added to my misery. The thrill of the big black 'bird' pulling up alongside me, the window sliding down an inch, allowing warm, aftershave laden air to waft out with the silken words 'Jump in' melted my knees.

Someone loved me! And so, for the next three hours, I was warm and dry. It was warm and dry for Ron, the observer, too. Too warm and dry!

So much so that his previous night of partying and whatever else, had caught up with him. His eyelids kept closing. For longer and longer periods. No matter how hard he tried he could not stop them closing.

Mick, the driver, noticed and gave both Ted, the operator, and myself a sly wink, as if to say, 'Get ready.'

We were driving down Wells Way and approaching a notorious humped back bridge over the canal when Mick hit the accelerator. Hard! The power of the 3.8 Jag shot us forward.

As we took off on the canal bridge, Mick roared some expletive, I haven't a clue what, but it frightened the life out of me. What it did to Ron, goodness only knows, but I was aware of his coming back to an extremely confused reality. He half shouted; half screamed as his head hit the roof lining. Arms and legs flailing madly as he tried to work out what was happening! As the car landed so did Ron—upside down in the floor well.

Mick calmly said, 'Damn pigeons,' and drove on.

Ron didn't sleep again.

Chapter Ten
Accidents. Accidents and More Accidents (Sometimes All at Once!)

It was a beautiful sunny Saturday afternoon and Alan and I were making our way to our respective beats, fifteen and sixteen; the most distant of all the beats at Costner Street.

In those days it was taboo to be even seen together on a beat, let alone walk together on it. One beat. One plodder. Never quite understood it personally, as it seemed to me that two blokes together were company for one another, therefore happier and more likely to work harder, plus the fact that they were protection for each other in nasty moments.

To me that seemed liked common sense, but no . . . one beat, one plodder.

How it worked would be: at some point during the tour of duty, you would be met, on the beat, by the station sergeant, who would sign your pocket book to prove you were where you should be, or, as the mobile phone hadn't yet been invented, the other way of 'proving-where-you-should-be' was by means of the 'ring in', i.e. a police box—better known as a Dr Who Tardis. (They were situated all over the area, normally on the extremity beats, the farthest points from the station, and, old fashioned as it may sound now, they had a phone! They were also a handy shelter in bad weather, plus they were a rest for sore feet, a place to write up your pocket book and, if you were lucky, perfect for eating fish and chips purloined along the way!)

Alan and I were wandering unaccosted together, simply because we were going the same way. So it was okay. Well I think it was. We never met a station sergeant so . . . Anyway, we were just approaching the Old Kent Road from Albany Road, when a guy passed us and said, 'Bit of an 'ows your father round the corner!'

Sure enough, as we turned the corner, there were two cars, one up the back end of the other at the traffic lights. Their respective drivers appeared to be having quite a contretemps, so we decided to intervene. However, we hadn't stepped off the kerb, when a third car came careering up the road and apparently not even braking, ran straight into the back of the second car with such force that it pushed its back end up in the air and came to stop underneath it.

I must say, the other drivers ceased their contretemps!

We were even more surprised when the third driver got out laughing, saying 'Oops!' and staggered all over the road! Out of his face, as the saying goes. The 'newt' had nothing on him. His breath was enough to inebriate me!

Alan and I were pleased to be double handed, so I went for the drunk driver while Alan attempted to placate the other two.

I had hardly reached my felon when there was a resounding crash behind me. I turned just in time to see a motorcyclist doing a perfect '10' somersault in mid-air before completing a passable rolling breakfall on the tarmac.

Amazingly, believe it or not, he didn't appear hurt as he got up and ran back to his bike—now buried in the side of a transit van. He shouted, 'My Bonny. My Bonny!'

His bike was, or should I say, had been, a beautiful Triumph Bonneville, now a considerably shortened version and in need of serious care and attention!

I know policemen are incredibly versatile and, dare I say it, superhuman beings, but they still have only one pair of hands!

Alan and I were no exception, and this latest issue would have to wait its turn!

So, feeling sorry for the motorcycle and van and not so much so for the inattentive motorcyclist, I shouted, 'Hang on, pal, we'll be with you in a mo'.'

The van driver gave me the thumbs up while the motorcyclist continued his wail, 'My Bonny. My Bonny!'

I turned back to deal with my drunk driver and was just in time to see a woman jumping into the road with a pushchair. The pushchair seriously tilted, but fortunately the infant within stayed put.

An interesting tirade flowed from the mum's lips (I think I'd heard most of the words used) directed at a bemused-looking lorry driver! I'm not sure why he was looking so bemused as, it transpired, he'd thought he could pass our melee by driving along the pavement!

Now pavements, as we all know, are for pedestrians and not 40-ton artics! Hence once the lorry had both nearside wheels on the footpath, it simply gave way, leaving all said wheels buried up to their axles in paving slabs and a big hole.

I didn't know whether to lie on my back and wave my legs in the air, blow bubbles, or sing 'Land of Hope and Glory'! As it was, Alan and I simply stared at each other thinking, 'Probably not a good time to go for a coffee break!' Interesting Saturday afternoon though.

At least the lady with her pushchair wandered off unscathed.

* * *

It wasn't long after this that I was called to another accident involving motorcycles, just farther along the Old Kent Road towards New Cross, at what was known as the Canal Bridge. It's easier to state in hindsight, what happened, rather than what I found on arrival.

Involved were two large motorcycles, one a Honda Gold Wing, the other a Kawasaki 900. Without going too much into motorcycle 'techi-stuff', suffice it to say that the series 1 Honda Gold Wing had a shaft driven 999 cc engine, whereas the Kawasaki had a transverse four-cylinder chain driven 903 cc engine.

Both were fast, but it was reported that the Gold Wings' top speed was 125 mph as opposed to the Kawasaki at 120 mph, but as the Gold Wing was a heavier bike its acceleration wasn't so quick. Compared to bikes of today, these speeds would be classed as positively 'tortoise', but in the day, the Kawasaki was probably the fastest road bike on sale.

According to an eye witness, these two had been stationary at red traffic lights on the New Cross side of the canal bridge facing central London, eyeing up each other's bike. No conversation had taken place but a 'let's see whose is fastest' communication had been non verbally given, as both riders began 'bleeping' their respective throttles and waiting for the lights to change.

It's important to state at this juncture that the seating position of both bikes was profoundly different in that the Gold Wing was more of a 'sit-up-like-a-gentleman' style compared to the 'head-down-backside-up' pose of the Kawasaki.

Hence as the lights flashed green, both bikes took off towards the bridge with the Gold Wing's rider at least seeing where he was going!

The canal bridge had quite a humped back, meaning that neither rider could see over the bridge as they commenced their would-be race off. As they topped the brow, the Honda rider, with the better sitting position, could see that 100 yards in front of them was a large Post Office depot to their left. What was worse was the fact that there was a PO box van in the process of turning into the site and was 90 degrees to the oncoming motorcycles and directly in their path.

The Honda immediately shut off his engine. The Kawasaki rider still had his head down and looked up only feet from the side of the van. By this point, it was estimated later, the 'connection speed' would have been around 70 mph.

A perfect image of the rider's face was visible in the soft aluminium side of the van. I don't think I need to say what I found at the scene. Suffice to say, I doubt the Gold Wing rider did much racing from then on. The Kawasaki rider certainly didn't.

Years later, as a member of the traffic division, I remember reporting on many accidents involving motorcyclists and, strangely enough, the amount involving large motorcycles could probably be counted on one hand. However, those involving smaller bikes with less mature riders . . . regrettably, I lost count.

Although today learner riders may only ride bikes up to 125 cc, back then, you were legally allowed to ride machines up to, and including, 250 cc. As technological improvements to engines grew, manufacturers were able to get much more torque and revs, and therefore road speed, out of less and less cubic centimetres.

So, what was all the fuss about, I hear you say?

Around that time, Yamaha brought out an RD250LC motorcycle. Absolutely nothing wrong with the bike. It was a good looking, reliable and very quick machine. The snag was, little Joe Soap could get off his pedal cycle, buy the 250LC and ride it . . . or try to! They didn't need any training unless they asked for it or wanted to pass a test.

As any rider will know the throttle (or accelerator) on a motorcycle is a twist grip on the right-hand side of the handlebar. The bike is stationary when it's in the off position. To gain speed, you simply 'twisted it'. Max revs (and ultimately speed) being gained with an approximately 40–45 degree 'twist' of the wrist on the grip. Not a lot! The skill is in knowing how much to 'twist it', and when!

The RD had the looks, character, and appeal to turn the heart of any young boy and instantly became the only object of desire for them and their mates. RD stood for race developed. Yamaha had a long racing history feeding their development, and RDs were raced in all sorts of different categories. They were lightweight and when you hit the powerband they took off like a scalded cat!

They were loud, annoying, brightly coloured, and dangerous. And old people complained about them! That was enough for the kids. They were hopelessly in love from first sight. To own an RD and ride it like an idiot was to be the coolest kid on the estate and became every kid's dream.

The RD250LC weighed in at 152 kg dry and produced 30 bhp as standard. That's a recipe for fun even today. Kawasaki's Ninja 250R offers pretty much the same power and weight in spite of being a four-stroke twin.

The character of the RD, and the typical owner, tended to be deliberately obnoxious, sticking two fingers up at pretty much everyone, dropping two gears and leaving them all coughing in a cloud of blue two-stroke smoke. That is, unfortunately, the usual nostalgic memory of past owners (at least the ones that lived). And their neighbours.

Maybe I'm being a bit harsh, but regrettably, the sensible 'kids' that rode them were very much in the minority!

So, who was/is to blame for the 'far too many' tragedies my colleagues and I had to deal with? For the bikes under lorries, the bikes in walls, the somersaulted bike that ended up on top of its rider because he'd twisted the throttle too fast.

The manufacturers for making such powerful bikes for learners?

The kids for being flash or refusing to get trained?

Parents for letting kids get them in the first place?

The government, etc. for not acting quicker to sort out the law?

Actually it's never any good attempting to ask who's to blame. The kids were ending up just as dead! And, anyway, if you point the finger, there's always three pointing back at you!

Many was the time at accidents that I remember standing beside the remains of yet another young life and thinking, 'I wish the manufacturers, parents, officials, and "tearaways" could be with me to see this.'

As I've said before, the beauty of the police force was its unpredictability. You simply didn't know what a day would bring forth. One day you'd have a kitten stuck up a tree and another the same tree would have fallen over a row of parked cars!

So it was in the world of accidents. One day you'd have an ultra-complicated multi-car pile up and the next . . . well let me tell you about one that took place in a bus lane.

It was a damp, dull, grey day. Devoid of all colour. Monochromed. A day that would have been much better spent curled up in bed. Although it wasn't actually raining, the greyness made you wet.

I was driving north along Brixton Road, feeling as damp as the day, when I saw some kind of commotion in the bus lane. Cars had been abandoned; buses appeared to have been strewn everywhere.

Chaos was probably a better word than *commotion*.

I parked up to find a car had meandered into the bus lane into the path of a bus. The snag was a bicycle had come between them. The bike was a total wreck, but fortunately the rider had been thrown clear. I say fortunately but make your own mind up – he'd gone over his handlebars and over the car bonnet, to land in the middle of the road. Thrown clear, yes, but in the process had bent his leg between the knee and ankle! The shin bone, at the break point, was almost protruding through the skin and was not being helped by a keen first aider.

Now, in my service, I've met some excellent first aiders, and some . . . not so excellent! This gentleman was definitely of the latter breed.

His left hand was on the patients' left thigh and his right

supporting his knee. This meant that the cyclists' lower leg was dangling at right angles to the rest of his leg! Not helped by the first-aider being down on his haunches, unbalanced and wobbling, thereby causing the already precariously positioned leg to swing!

In my best non-panicked, non-screaming voice, I said, 'What are you doing?'

Without batting an eyelid, he said, 'I'm a fully qualified first aider. Please leave this to me.'

I happened to be a member of our divisional first aid team and I knew that, in competition at least, when approaching an incident you said loudly and clearly, 'I'm a fully qualified first aider. What has happened here?'

What indeed? What I was witnessing beggared belief. How the bone did not penetrate the skin, I'll never know, but fortunately the ambulance arrived just at that point and were able to use words I wasn't allowed to use, and some I'd never heard of, to relieve the first aider of his duties!

Fortunately the rider was out of it. Knocked out in the collision or through the shear pain of his ordeal, I don't know, but I left him to the professionals.

I took statements and dealt with everything else thinking, 'If I ever find myself in that situation (hopefully not!) but if I did . . . how would I react if I heard those immortal words, 'I'm a fully qualified first aider. What has happened here?'

Chapter Eleven
Motorbikes

It was around this time that something fell into my lap that was to initiate a very pleasant period in my police career. Two years in fact.

When I made a report on the street, for example, a motorist crossing a junction against a red light, a process or enquiry was set in motion.

Process route:

1. Offence committed on the street. Report made.
2. Report goes to administration and prepared for court.
3. Court.

Number 2, administration, is where the driver's documents are checked, or statements are taken, or firms are reported for offences committed by the vehicles owned as opposed to driver error; anything required to give a successful prosecution at court.

These enquiries were carried out, not surprisingly, by enquiry officers, and in the Met in those days there was a department called the Enquiry Unit.

The unit for my division was moving to another building and, in the process, had found that there were many outstanding reports left undone. Namely, difficult, awkward ones.

That is to say that many of these reports ended up with requests for beat bobbies to complete. Rather than hand them out they were left for the men to take and complete as and when. Many officers loathed it. I enjoyed it. It meant a very pleasant hour spent in someone's house taking a statement with a cup of tea and a biscuit.

The only problem was that many of these reports had originally been left because of either their complexity or simply because the drivers could not be found and, after a while, the more difficult enquiries got left altogether.

I noticed that eventually there was a substantial pile left that no-one wanted to touch and, as I said, I enjoyed them. Thus it was that I approached my shift inspector and offered my services to attack the pile. I didn't realise what a blessing I was or what an embarrassment it had been for him in the fact that they were not getting completed.

He immediately said, 'The jobs yours. Take the next month off for it. Do whatever shifts you like and if at the end of that time there are more to do, you can have more time.'

The lads thought I'd taken leave of my senses; hassle, hassle and more hassle were their thoughts. My thoughts were all my birthdays had come at once! No more shifts for what one, two months? Who knew? It actually turned into two years! I could go to parties whenever I wanted and knew I didn't have to get up the next day! No earlies, lates, or nights, unless I said so, or it was necessary for the completion of a job in hand. Fantastic!

It was hard work, and I did work hard, but thoroughly enjoyed every minute of it. In the end I was left with around a dozen that would never be completed, either the offenders were deceased, or buildings had been flattened or some other such reason.

'You've actually enjoyed that, haven't you?' my shift inspector said, as I returned them to him, one morning. 'You've done a job nobody wanted and saved my neck into the bargain. Well done!'

I felt ten-foot-tall! Everybody likes a bit of encouragement, especially when it comes from the boss. 'I've got to admit I did,' I said. 'I met some very interesting people. Some nice, some not so nice. Some downright horrendous. But, yes, I've thoroughly enjoyed it, and I'm actually sorry its finished.'

He turned round and picked up a letter from the administration chief inspector—in those days anybody above inspector was a God—never seen by the likes of mere minions like me!

He précised its contents to me, but basically it was offering me a job in their department, with an area of the division of my own! As the work entailed a lot of foot slogging, I was to be sent on a motorcycle course with immediate effect and was to start with the department as soon as such course had been taken, if I wished to accept.

If I wished to accept? Motorcycle course doing the job which, for the last two months, had been a single man's dream. I almost kissed him!

Of course, it did mean passing the motorcycle course first. Normally, in civvy street one would have an instructor once or twice a week for an hour or so at a time, with a test several weeks on. This was to be a two-week intensive nine to five, five days a week, course at Hendon. I lived in Greenwich. Opposite ends of London. Hour and a half travelling each way, every day.

Just like earlies, I had to be up and leave the section house (a purpose-built building of many floors for single PCs) by 6.00 am to be at Hendon in North London for 9.00 am. As I said, I hated early turn, well the getting up for it anyway, but for a motorcycle course . . . a hardship? Not on your life. Funny how the mind and the body work when it's something you really want to do!

It took most of the first morning to kit us out with boots, gloves, helmet, and gear. I'd been looking forward to this and imagining myself dressed to impress in leathers, boots, and a full-face, tinted visor!

Didn't turn out quite like that. The boots were great, but the helmet was an adaptation of the street helmet, just made of sterner stuff with a strap. Different, but okay. The leathers were not leather. A one-piece raincoat with crutch flap, commonly known as a 'gabardine nappy'. Once the coat was put round the shoulder and buttoned on the inside, this flap was pulled up between the legs and buttoned into place, hence 'nappy', before final buttoning and belting. The overall ensemble was not really the look I'd been expecting.

Being gaberdine, it kept you fairly dry except for riding in heavy rain. The flap formed a sort of saucer in the lap, which collected water quite dramatically and, like any saucer, when full of liquid it overflowed—onto the crutch! A real nappy would have been an asset; this simply led to a somewhat of an uncomfortable day. One learnt very quickly not to go out in the rain unless absolutely necessary.

The first afternoon was getting used to the machine.

Not the 650 cc Triumphs I'd seen police riding in town, but a Velocette 200 cc liquid cooled extravaganza! A sort of cross between a motorcycle and a scooter, and not the most powerful machines in the world but I was determined to put my 'surprises' (uniform, bikes!) to one side and enjoy the course.

And enjoy it I did. Getting used to the machine meant doing things on it I would never have deemed possible. I thought we were being trained for the circus. Standing up while moving; standing up with no hands while moving; standing on the seat while moving; standing on one leg on the seat while moving. All done on the off-road Hendon aerodrome I might add! I can't imagine what the public would have thought seeing a squad of policemen riding down the Mall standing on one leg on the seat of a motorcycle-cum-scooter, wearing nappies!

But it worked. The bike became a part of us. You felt that anything you could do on your legs, you could do on the bike.

We were all beginners, and it was important to spend time off-road getting used to stopping, starting, negotiating bollards, even getting the bike on and off its stand; all the usual things that are necessary before they were going to let us loose on the open road.

And then the day arrived; we were let loose. Look out motorists, here we come.

We were put into groups of three with our Velocettes and an instructor on a 650 Saint. The intensive off-road training was now holding us in good stead. Careful but stable. Slowly we were taken onto wider, faster roads until we were naturally blending with the other traffic and travelling at speeds that were commensurate with everyone else.

I mentioned earlier that the Velocette was not the speediest of motorcycles, and this was particularly the case when carrying loads, by which I mean, riders of size!

Now I wasn't huge, but I was bigger than my two compatriots. This meant that for me to keep up, I had to keep the bike wound up in third gear. This meant holding the throttle wide open. The second I attempted to put it into top, the revs dropped right off, together with my speed, and I was left for dead, watching my mates disappearing into the distance and poor old Gertrude, as I lovingly called my Velocette, wheezing for breath!

Keeping it wound up wasn't a problem, except for petrol consumption! Because of the extra effort the poor thing was having to go through, I was running out of 'juice' twice as fast as the others and therefore not quite reaching designated fuelling stops.

My instructor had an idea.

'What's that?' I said, feeling a little fed up and embarrassed that I was keeping the others back.

'Next time they disappear into the distance, you're in for the ride of your life. We'll show 'em!'

I had no idea what he was talking about, and before I could formulate a question, he'd disappeared into the distance. I was getting used to inhaling exhaust fumes and being sprayed with gravel from accelerating motorcycle tyres.

However, I was about to find to find out what he was on about. They say that hindsight's a wonderful thing. If I'd had even some in these circumstances, I'm not sure I would have hung around to take the motorcycle test anyway!

As per usual, two or three hours into the ride, I was finding it difficult to keep up. I was trying my hardest. I had my head down, tail up, throttle fully open, and poor old Gertrude straining at the gunnels. Suddenly I became aware of my instructor pulling up alongside.

'You'll feel a slight improvement to your speed in a second,' he shouted over the engine scream. 'Don't worry. Just steer and enjoy.'

He slowly slotted in behind me. I was still struggling to know what he was talking about, when I suddenly felt his boot rest on the rear of my seat.

In panic, his plan burst upon me. Newton's third law of physics was about to become real to me—'every action elicits an equal and opposite reaction'. I was going to get a push with a 650 cc Triumph motorcycle! I didn't know whether to laugh, cry, or jump off. As it was, I could do nothing.

My speed was increasing by the second. Until now, all I'd ever experienced was 30 mph, soaring up to 34 when I'd been going downhill, even up to a face-stretching 36 if I'd had a tail wind!

Those speeds came and went as Newton's law took over and I crossed the 40 barrier. 50. 60! As 70 loomed I realised the 'gaberdine nappy' I was wearing wasn't just to catch rain!

The other members of my group were now in sight and I was rapidly catching up. As I roared past them, I don't know who was most shocked, me, them, or Gertrude!

Fortunately, before my nappy got too full, I saw a petrol station ahead. The speed began to drop off and I slowly pulled onto the forecourt. My hands were seized to the handlebars and my face frozen in a rictus of pure panic. I couldn't move.

My instructor pulled alongside and said, 'I told you we'd show 'em!' and then left me to fill up—fill what? The bike—yes. Anything else—a bit late, I thought.

I got to the end of the course and managed to pass, although I still have sleepless nights about that ride. But what a great course.

Chapter Twelve
A New Office With My Own Desk!

Complete with my fresh, gleaming motorcycle licence, goggles, helmet, and boots—oh, yes—and my gaberdine nappy, freshly cleaned, I joined the enquiry team two weeks later.

I'm sure that there will be people who are wondering why a young bloke should give up the excitement of the street for a random office job involving the taking of statements and pen pushing? Well, that's understandable, and it certainly wasn't through boredom. The police force may be a lot of things, but being boring certainly isn't one of them! I loved the street work and never knowing what a day would bring was exciting enough, but it must be borne in mind that the unpredictable, exhilarating, unexpected occurrences I've been talking about don't happen all the time. There's a lot of wandering around, asking questions, giving directions, getting wet, cold and weary. But that notwithstanding, I enjoyed every day, it's just that a change is as good as a rest, and I fancied a change.

Therefore, bright, and breezy that first Monday morning, I found myself in a room with eight other enquiry officers and Frank, our office manager, plus . . . a desk for me! My *own* desk. I'd never had one.

Before my cadet days, the first sixteen years of my life had been spent in an idyllic Lake District village in a two-hundred-year-old cottage with two bedrooms, a sitting room, kitchen and loo, beside a wood (mini forest really). Absolutely idyllic, but small. No bathroom, certainly no office, and absolutely certainly no desk, only a small drop leaf table for eating off. Therefore, floor space only for homework (or mam's dressing table at exam time).

I ought to say that, although we had no bathroom, we did bathe! In a four-foot zinc one in front of the fire on a Friday night. Yes, Friday night was bath night. Me first, being the eldest, my kid brother next, then, after we'd gone to bed, Mam, and finally Dad. (Or so I'm told!) Another world. But still, idyllic.

And now, here I was, with my own desk . . . and an overflowing 'in' basket! So exciting. I couldn't wait to get started.

After sorting everything out into some semblance of order—important, urgent, urgent but not important, important but not urgent—yes, as always, it fell into one pile, urgent and important! Don't they always. Basically, my sorting was into street order.

Hence, armed with my brand-new clipboard, complete with enquiries, map, my carry-file, and no gaberdine nappy (it was a beautiful day) I set off on my first sojourn. Sadly, I had no fanfare, cortège or even waving hankies from my other colleagues, can't understand why, or maybe I can. It took me twenty minutes to leave the yard; bike wouldn't start! The first of many, many . . . many times, it was to happen over the months. Rather than hanky waving I think the other guys, knowing what was to happen, were hiding.

Anybody who has ever been fortunate enough to own one of these Velocette contraptions knows the procedure one has to go through to get them started when the kick start fails. Second gear; run as fast as possible, with the bike of course, until maximum momentum is achieved; slip the clutch, and then jump on side saddle to give purchase to the rear wheel. Hopefully—so long as you don't unbalance and go base over apex, or the bike doesn't take off without you—it starts. Usually, first time; if it didn't then the procedure had to be repeated until success was achieved.

I was to learn that some bikes were better than others and first come, first served, meant that one could get a better bike. That had to be done immediately on arrival at work, of course. Before anything else. On this occasion, I was last to get a bike. Hence, twenty minutess late leaving.

I'd attempted to memorise the route I should take before leaving the office, but being new and unfamiliar with the area, I kept forgetting either the street or the number of flat/house I needed. This meant stopping to look. I very rapidly learnt not to switch the engine off while doing so . . . for reasons aforementioned!

After three or four hours I had completed just two enquiries. By the end of my tour I had completed three! Another lesson learnt—make appointments and get your timing right before you go out. Teething problems! Still, it had been a beautiful day for poodling around the streets of London on two wheels.

I slowly got into the swing of a new regime, with new mates, in a new job, and continued to have a whale of a time.

I also learnt how to organise my time, with clients mainly. Some you enjoyed sitting and chatting with and having a nice cup of tea. Others you couldn't get away from quick enough, for various reasons. People with verbal diarrhoea who wanted to tell you their life stories; some who hadn't washed their cups in a month; aromas from curry to unwashed bodies and worse which caressed your nostrils to the point of nausea . . . Just think of an encounter-cum-meetup that has caused you to want to scream or run a mile and you'll get the times to which I'm referring.

But, as I said, sometimes there are very interesting people with whom you want to spend some time and chat.

One such was a guy, a little older than me, who enjoyed wine making. He'd witnessed an accident and I'd been given the enquiry to obtain a statement. I suppose statements made up around 50 per cent of my work and were normally extremely interesting, either the story itself or the person from whom you were receiving the story.

On entering his flat one couldn't fail to notice that his hobby was wine making. All around the room were demijohns in various degrees of fermentation, bubbling and popping.

Conversation very rapidly came round to the topic of wine-making as he pointed out what concoction was in each jar. Pear, cucumber, potato, hawthorn, rose, dandelion leaf—in fact, very much anything that grew above or below the ground could be stuck in a bottle and turned into wine—and I mean anything.

One he pointed to was apparently made from rice and he told me an old girlfriend of his, who had been of Chinese origin, thought it was saki. I'd never tasted saki and on sampling this brew, was quite glad.

I was quite enjoying the 'sampling', as he went through the sweet, sour, dark and lights of the vegetable wine, fruit wine, hedgerow wine—I'm sure you're getting the picture—when he came to one which he referred to as his rubbish wine.

'Obviously that's one that hasn't worked,' I said. 'Why keep it?'
'Taste it,' he said.

By now, they were all beginning to taste very enjoyable. Even the saki would have tasted good. But as soon as this golden nectar touched my lips, I knew why he had that supercilious, very-pleased-with-himself look on his face. 'Good, isn't it?'

It was the most delicious fluid ever to grace my throat! 'What in the world is that?' I crooned, 'and why call it rubbish? It's amazing!'

'Well, it was an experiment, actually. One Sunday when I'd finished preparing the Sunday dinner, I was just about to throw the potato peelings, cabbage scrunts, and carrot scratchings on the compost, when I thought, 'I wonder what sort of wine that would make? And voila! Bob's your uncle!' (Scrunts, by the way are cabbage stalks. My dad was born and bred on the hills of West Cumberland, and I can only assume it's a Cumbrian word.)

That's what I was drinking. His rubbish wine was absolutely delicious. 'You need to get that patented, or at the very least approach Sainsburys and ask for a sub,' I said. He thought it was a joke, but I really don't think he knew what a fantastic product he'd stumbled upon!

He started to move to another bottle until I stopped him and suggested we take his statement before I was unable to see the page. Needless to say, a half- to three-quarter-of-an-hour statement needs some refreshment and neither of us felt like tea so . . . When I'd finished, I got up to go and realised I had a Velocette parked outside! There was no way I was going to ride it back to the office and asked if I could push it into his garage until the morning when I would be better placed to ride it back. He agreed, but I made him promise he wouldn't offer me any more wine on collection!

Back at the office, I piled my one statement into my basket and caught a bus home. The next morning, after a chat and catch up on life, I started to do some paper work. When I came to the previous night's statement, I couldn't believe my eyes and rapidly covered it with a book, shiftily glancing around the room to see if anyone had noticed. Not only was it illegible, but none of it was on the line! It looked more like Picasso's attempt at drawing a stormy sea!

I had to collect my motorcycle anyway, so, armed with new statement papers, I hot footed it back to my wine vendor! Believe it or not, he did offer me another wine, this time in a bottle. The rubbish wine—as a memento. I kept it for some time before drinking it. I was sorely tempted to visit Sainsburys.

The job was great, but I did have a love–hate relationship with the Velocette. I made up my mind one windy, dull, but dry day in March! I'd had a great day, enquiry wise, having completed twelve to fourteen jobs. A real mixture of firms, statements, and HORT 1 enquiries. The latter were always tricky, they were the forms issued on the street by officers to people who didn't have documentation with them and who had failed to turn up at a police station of their choice within the stipulated time. Many were fine; just a matter of forgetting. But there were also those who had no documents and/ or had given false names and addresses, or worse, that hadn't come to light at the time. This meant I had to do quite a lot of further enquiry work trying to find the culprits. Then it was something of a cat and mouse game trying to catch them, either at home or work, at a family or friend's address, on the street, or in a car! Anywhere a human could hide, or simply be, was where I had to look! All part of my days' work, and this day's work had been, as I said, a good one—until I tried to start my bike!

I'd been slow in getting to work that day and all the best bikes were gone. It meant that more than once on this trip I had had to do my gaberdine nappy dance with the bike. Run, jump, bounce. Run, jump, bounce. Run . . . Much to the enjoyment of onlookers.

Of course, many of the areas in which I had to go through this façade were not the most salubrious places, they were the places where most of the onlookers were the very people who I'd been looking for and been unable to find, they therefore thoroughly enjoyed the spectacle, and didn't offer a hand because they were hoping that this lunatic policeman would end up in an unceremonious heap! It should be said that not all villains live in such places, but quite a lot do. There are good and bad in all walks of life. It just happened that my area contained quite a lot of the undesirables. Fortunately, I had ended my day with a statement in a nice neighbourhood—one of the few on my patch, when the bike played up again. Wouldn't start. I put my papers on top of a nearby postbox and went through my rigmarole.

Run, jump, bounce. Run . . . I was so excited when it fired the first time that, before I gave it a chance to change its mind, I roared off back to the police station. I walked into my office and went through the motions of placing my papers in my basket, only to realise—no papers. Still on the post box!

I think the bike was feeling sorry for me and started first time as I returned to the site of the misdemeanour. When I arrived back at the scene—I did say it was dry, dull *and windy*, didn't I?—my papers were scattered from one end of the street to the other.

It was dry, but hadn't been, which meant that there were some muddy puddles and patches which, fortunately, had trapped some papers. Covered them with mud, but held them. Others had been blown into the road and cars had held them, or attempted to, with their tyres, forming beautiful patterns across my copperplate, hand-scripted statements. Most, however, were still blowing in the wind.

Hard as it may be to believe, I retrieved every document! Only one statement was past the point of no return and that was by a delightful lady who saw the funny side of it and was prepared to give me another one. I probably got through a few erasers that day trying to eradicate mud and tyre marks from the reports but, overall, I got off light!

You can be sure I didn't make the same mistake again! Report taken, onto clip board, into carrying case, into bike pannier, then, and only then, run, jump, bounce. Run, jump . . . ! That was one of the occasions when I found it easy to decide which side of the love–hate relationship I fell into with the bike!

There was no doubt about it, I loved this phase of my police career, but I realised if I became too content, I'd never want to move. The gentle shove I needed to make the move came in a roundabout, rather tragic, savage way. Frank, our office manager, and long-term police sergeant, was one of those true gentlemen we all felt was indispensable. Regardless of what time we started work, he would almost always be there. No matter what time we finished, he would almost certainly still be there! If we were stuck on a legal issue or any other sort of issue, Frank had the answer. If we'd dropped a clanger, we'd get the biggest b——g of our lives and then have him sort it for us without repercussion or fallout. He was the gaffer, no doubt about it, but we, to a man, would trust him with our lives. Totally indispensable.

I came in one Monday morning—no Frank!

'Two of us in before Frank,' said Alf, another old-time PC who had been in the department since the year dot. 'First time in fifteen years I've beaten him in!'

One by one the other lads came in, but no Frank.

Around ten o'clock, the big boss came in. 'Sorry lads. Bad news. Frank had a massive heart attack over the weekend. Didn't make it.' He was unable to say more and, red-eyed, he left the office.

They'd been almost closer than brothers. They had started the job on the same day. Followed each other round the force and were both looking forward to a long retirement with their wives. Frank had just turned fifty.

What were we going to do? We all just sat staring at one another. Lost for words. We hadn't just lost our gaffer, but our mentor, supporter, friend . . . Nobody could ever replace Frank.

We returned just after lunch to find Kevin sitting in Frank's seat. A jovial, friendly, long-term sergeant very similar to Frank in many ways. Slightly younger, but apparently every bit as competent. By booking off time everything was, again, running smoothly.

An old poem by Saxon White Kessinger came to mind.

INDISPENSABLE MAN

Sometime when you're feeling important;
Sometime when your ego's in bloom
Sometime when you take it for granted
You're the best qualified in the room,

Sometime when you feel that your going
Would leave an unfillable hole,
Just follow these simple instructions
And see how they humble your soul;

Take a bucket and fill it with water,
Put your hand in it up to the wrist,
Pull it out and the hole that's remaining
Is a measure of how you'll be missed.

You can splash all you wish when you enter,
You may stir up the water galore,
But stop and you'll find that in no time
It looks quite the same as before.

The moral of this quaint example
Is do just the best that you can,
Be proud of yourself but remember,
There's no indispensable man.

Chapter Thirteen
CID Material Not in the Making

I left the Enquiry Unit with mixed feelings. Sad but with no regrets. I'd made many new friends, had a thoroughly enjoyable time, and learnt a new aspect of the job into the bargain.

There's an old saying: 'If you always do what you always did, you'll always get what you always got!' I wanted more. I wanted the Traffic Department really badly, and yet I could feel the comfort, enjoyment, and suffocating delight of the Enquiry Unit biting deep. I was sinking into a lethargic time warp from which, if I didn't rouse myself, the self-induced coma would self-inducingly suffocate me!

Time to move on. So, I returned to Costner Street. and back onto beat work for a while until I could apply for Traffic.

There has always been a confusion in people's minds that CID and uniform are two totally different worlds where 'Never the twain shall meet'. In actual fact, our CID colleagues are simply uniformed police officers that don't wear uniforms and have specialised in crime.

The uniformed beat bobby dealt with anything and everything coming his way, including crime, until the crime became too involved and needed the expertise of the specialists, at which time it would be handed over to the CID. Not because the uniformed officer was inadequate, but simply because more time and 'sleuthing' was probably required than the beat man was able to give. Added to this, of course, was the fact that the beat man had not received the extensive training in the disciplines required for CID work.

Specialising in any department, from the dog section to horse branch, or CID to traffic, only came after the first two years probationary period (those first two years out of training school) after which time you had a much better 'handle' on which direction you wanted your career to take. I knew mine was towards Traffic, but that didn't mean I didn't like super-sleuthing as well! Lots of crime, and police work in general, came from motor vehicles anyway.

Most villains used cars to get from A to B as well as using them as get-away vehicles. Regrettably, the majority of these type of people had such little respect for the law that maintaining a vehicle or obtaining correct documentation was simply an inconvenience and not necessary! Driving disqualifications didn't count either, hence simply stopping a vehicle in the street could lead to, well, anything.

It was on one such occasion that I stopped an old Humber Super Snipe. They were lovely old cars, well made and quite luxurious inside, but expensive to buy, keep, and maintain. Normally one found men with trilby hats and smoking pipes behind the wheel (or am I pigeonholing?). Therefore, seeing a young, rather unsavoury character at the wheel on this particular day gave me the old 'gut' feeling that something wasn't quite right, and further scrutiny was necessary. I stopped him and the normal general chat took place:

'Is this your car?'

'Yes.'

'Nice car. How long have you had it?'

'A few weeks.'

'Expensive to run?'

On and on we went until I started to look round the vehicle and found three bald tyres, no windscreen wiper on the passenger side, no indicators, no horn, and brakes decidedly dodgy.

'Mmm,' I said, 'very expensive to run!'

'I know I've got some work to do but I have an MOT' and proceeded to produce said MOT. 'The guy I bought it from said it had just been done.'

The MOT was dated about two months previously. I felt that there was no way the vehicle could deteriorate to its current state in such a short time and my gut feeling grew. He was unable to show me any other documents, nor could he verify his ownership of the vehicle or his name and address. We therefore returned to the police station together, where further enquiries could be made in comfort. Little did I know the route those enquiries would lead me on.

It turned out that the MOT belonged to a book of MOTs stolen from a garage several months earlier. Several books, actually. If I could trace back through the owners of the vehicle and discover at what point that MOT came into their hands . . . The sleuth was on!

The vehicle had changed hands no less than five times in that short period, and hence my enquiries led me to four different owners until I actually got to the chap who had, allegedly, had it MOTed.

Eventually I gleaned that a mate of a mate knew a garage, who knew a garage (you know the sort of thing!) where MOTs could be got without any questions asked. Much discussion, together with the legal aspects of his actions, led to not a few tears and court appearances . . . but I got the garage name and realised it wasn't far from our area. (It should be borne in mind, however, that although this has only taken a few short paragraphs to relate, it took in the region of four weeks to play out as it had to be fitted in between other duties and life in general.) I suppose I should have handed it over to CID earlier, as they had unlimited time to investigate, but I was enjoying myself, and anyway there was no rush.

That afternoon I informed my sergeant of what I'd been doing and what I was about to do. He told me not to do anything daft and to call in assistance if required.

I left the station and casually wandered over to where the 'dodgy' garage was purported to be, intending to just to take a look. I was in high spirits, adrenaline pumping with the thought of what was to transpire. I was about to make the greatest bust Costner Street had ever seen . . . Or something like that!

The garage was situated in a railway arch just off a fairly narrow, seedy, nondescript, dog muck, tin can and rubbish-infested road. Had it got darker or was I imagining it? As I approached, I became aware of a silence descending upon the area. Hammers stopped hammering, grinders stopped grinding, blow torches stopped blowing; even the traffic noise seamed to stop. My gut started talking to me again, 'Watch it, JT'; 'Be ready, JT'; 'Summats amiss, JT.'

In the doorway of the garage in question stood a broken-nosed, 300 lb gent, whose head almost touched the door lintel. Now taking a door lintel to be around seven-foot high, it meant this guy was either on a ladder or . . . Big! No ladder was in sight, and I therefore assumed, correctly, that he was big. Six-foot-six at least, with his overalls stretching to the limit around his shoulders, chest, and thighs. Certainly not over his stomach, that was pure six pack!

My mind went back to an old song about 'Big John':

> Sorta wide at the shoulder
> And narrow at the hip.
> And everyone knew
> You didn't give no lip
> To big John
> Big John
> Big, bad John.

Bearing in mind I was an ex-Cumberland and Westmorland rugby player, schoolboy shot champion, blue belt in Judo, and Metropolitan Police training school's wrestling champ—it was no contest.

He was bigger than me.

He definitely looked fitter than me.

I could see several pairs of eye-whites staring out at me from the gloom of the garage interior and . . . He was tapping a spanner, a very large spanner, into the palm of his right hand!

Now I'm no chicken, but the old proverb 'Discretion being the better part of valour' came to mind, I don't know why, and so I carried on wandering past them. (Well I did say I'd just gone down to take a look! And my sergeant had said not to do anything daft!)

I gave a good spurious look at them, of course, as I passed; it would have been expected and I didn't want to raise their suspicions, did I? As soon as I turned the corner, I immediately called for backup and explained the situation.

It was a wonderful sight to see a van load of mates turn up within minutes and an even more wonderful sight to see boxes of paperwork, including MOT books, number plates without cars, cars without number plates, bits of cars, motorcycles, bits of motorcycles, and several gents from the premises in handcuffs, including my spanner toting friend, come filing out!

It turned out that the premises had long been thought to be involved in vehicle crimes of all sorts, and only needed the slightest of footholds to bring about the search and subsequent result. Pretty successful, I thought!

It almost changed my mind from Traffic to CID but . . . not quite!

Chapter Fourteen
Holidays

Yes, we were given time off for good behaviour. All we had to do was make sure we booked holidays, or vacations, in good time.

Being a young sprog and single meant that school holidays or vacations were generally reserved for the family men who got first bite at the rota-cherry. Not a problem for me as I preferred to take my holidays when there were fewer members of the public about anyway.

What is the difference between a holiday and a vacation anyway? Wikipedia says:

> A holiday is a day set aside by custom or by law on which normal activities, especially business or work including school, are suspended, or reduced. Generally, holidays are intended to allow individuals to celebrate or commemorate an event or tradition of cultural or religious significance.

Whereas:

> A vacation is a leave of absence from a regular job, or a specific trip or journey, usually for the purpose of recreation or tourism. People often take a vacation during specific holiday observances, or for specific festivals or celebrations. Vacations are often spent with friends or family.

So there you have it . . . I think . . . are they saying the same thing or is it me that's thick? Do they say vacation in the US and holiday in the UK? Do you know there are some people, somewhere, who are paid megabucks to research that? And does it matter anyway?

Not sure why I've gone into all that . . . Whatever . . . I was going back to Gods' own country, Cumberland, for a well-earned rest! It was late winter and the Christmas period had just finished. Not terribly eventful from a job point of view but for a single bloke, very eventful!

I needed a rest and mid-January was perfect. Cold, frosty, dark nights, Mum's cooking! Well there had to be some positives. A couple of weeks from the end of a night-duty stretch was ideal.

I only took four days annual leave but managed to get twelve days off. I know it sounds weird but that was one of the positives about shift work in those days, if you worked it right. After night duty one generally got four days off (rostered weekly leave) before late turn. Therefore, adding time off (which was time accrued from overtime not taken off) meant that four days' annual leave plus five days off (i.e. forty hours) just before three days off (the next weekly leave cycle) meant a total of twelve days and, to boot, back onto late turn (which was three o'clock) meant I could travel in the morning from home, maybe take a couple more hours off that day starting at five o'clock.

I know . . . I've lost you . . . suffice to say I had nearly a fortnight off for the grand total of four days' annual leave . . . I'd worked it right!

I took four more hours off that night to give me an early start for Cumberland. I was in my trusty canary-coloured Ford Popular 100 E and needed as much help as possible. Not the fastest car on the road (40 mph tops—and that was downhill with a following wind!) and certainly not the most comfortable, and I did want to get back within the twelve days!

I'd managed to traverse London, it was around 3.00 am and I

was gaily travelling up the A1 (no M1 in those days, but a good road nonetheless with stretches of dual track periodically). The heater worked a treat—warm as toast. The early starters hadn't ventured out so the roads were quiet, peaceful in fact. My car wasn't modern enough to sponsor a radio, so I entertained myself by singing, whistling, trying to count the cat's eyes, etc!

It's a known fact that counting sheep is a soporific pastime, best thing in the world for sleep inducement. So imagine what effect the cat's eyes had on this lonely, tired, Cumberland-bound copper! Whatever possessed me to think I could count the cat's eyes anyway, even at my sedentary speed!

Suddenly the blur of cat's eyes turned into a continuous yellow smudge. The car began to rattle furiously as my off-side wheels crossed them and there in front of me, was no longer a yellow blur but the flashing lights of an oncoming car's main beam. There were no crash barriers back then and I'd crossed into the fast lane of London-bound traffic.

Believe me, nothing wakes you up quicker than headlights in your lane—or not being in your lane! I swerved frantically to my left, thankfully missing the oncoming car, but mounting the grass verge on my nearside.

My brain was in overload. Just as I was being lulled into a warm cat's eyes-induced slumber, I'd been confronted by a madman with headlamps far too bright for his car not liking my being in his lane going the wrong way! Strange man!

Not only that but the road builders had deliberately narrowed the A1 at this point causing me to mount the verge. The smell in the car was unbearable.

There was nothing behind me and the sole trouble maker's rear lights were slowly disappearing towards London. I stopped the car, got out, and filled my lungs with 4.00 am January air! Definitely better than the air in my car and no doubt the air in the other driver's car.

Poor chap! No doubt he was in a similar soporific stupor to myself and must have thought all his birthdays had come at once when he'd been confronted with a maniac coming towards him in his lane. Thank you, whoever you were, for not swerving into what should have been my lane. (And for not being as far gone as me!)

I'm going 'sixpence-half-crown' now, just remembering the incident. (I'll leave you to work out what 6d-2/6d means .Showing my age 6d-2/6d!)

Being tired when driving is as bad, if not worse, than drinking and driving. Believe me. I know. Don't do it! I parked up and had a nap.

Whilst writing this story I was reminded of another time when I was equally as moronic! It wasn't following a night duty and I wasn't tired, but it was a similar time of year. Mid-January and about mid-afternoon.

I'd sold my little canary-yellow bombshell and bought a Cortina Mk 1. Extremely posh and very comfortable, very reliable, but possibly even slower than the Pop! Maybe not. Anyway 50 mph was tanking it! I was again travelling up the A1 and again it was cold. Very cold, and in my mind, I could hear my dad saying 'On cold days, watch out for black ice. You'll see the frost on the road and know it can be slippy, but the black ice you won't see. Lethal.'

I'd got used to 50 mph. Got used to lorries passing me, all the time! So you can imagine how I felt when there, in front of me, was a lorry travelling slower than I was. Suddenly I was no longer driving a Mk 1 Cortina but a Lotus Cortina! (Every boy's dream car at the time.) I double de-clutched and slotted down a gear! Nothing behind me, so I pulled out and roared past him. (Well, not roaring exactly but you get the idea.)

I looked up at him as I passed, expecting him to be in awe of this gleaming beauty, but, in fact, just in time to see him pointing through his window at the road in front of him. Too late.

As I continued the overtake, I suddenly found myself pirouetting. My car was no longer heading for Carlisle and home, but back towards London, and I was facing the lorry driver who was calmly watching this young lunatic doing the fandango in his 'gleaming beauty' and no doubt slowing, thinking he was going to have to pick up the pieces.

My car, although I had my foot hard on the brake, was taking no notice of me whatsoever and continued its flawless dance until I was once again facing Carlisle. No, Manchester. No, the lorry driver again! Fortunately, my car had slewed onto the grass verge and was slowly coming to rest. The lorry driver passed and gave me a thumbs up.

Cheeky bloke. I'd like to have seen him twirl in his artic!

'—the black ice you won't see. Lethal!

Needless to say, in those days I hadn't learnt cadence braking (the rapid application of the footpedal when skidding) or driving with due consideration to the road conditions, or the fact that many times dads know best.

Looking back, lots of things my dad said make sense now.

Part Two

Traffic

Chapter Fifteen
Back to Driving School

Joining a new department meant I was becoming a specialist. I was still a uniformed police officer and, although I was no longer expected to carry out the duties of a beat officer, I was still a police officer but with traffic duties instead of those on the beat. I was now specialising in traffic—that meant all aspects of traffic: traffic jams, accidents, large loads and ambulances, defective vehicles. Anything traffic orientated was down to us. In order to do that, lots of training was needed. Lots and lots!

To start with, I wouldn't be walking about any longer (thank the stars!). To deal with the aforementioned issues, I would now be on two or four wheels. Firstly, two. In the Met, it was a progression to move to four. I wasn't bothered. Two wheels would be fine because I knew it would now be 650 cc solo motorcycles and not the dreaded Velocettes!

(I must be fair to old Gertrude, apart from pushing her more than riding her, she had served her purpose well and, dare I say—out of her presence and hearing, of course, and because she evoked such great memories—I held quite a soft spot for her!)

However, now it was big boys' toys! But first it was back to training school, or rather driving school; Triumph 650s were powerful, heavy, and very fast beasts; I had to learn how to ride them!

Of course, there was more to it than just riding. That meant studying (in depth) the highway code, road craft, nuts and bolts (i.e.

vehicle examining) and so on. All part of becoming a specialist, and aid to the man on the street.

New uniform. Fantastic. This time full leathers, surely? Not on your life, it was yet another gaberdine nappy. We did get new helmets though! Not full face, but proper helmet and goggles at least

After the Velocette, and not knowing anything else, 'beast' was a good name, i.e. 450 cc more to start with and only me and two wheels to pull. They were quick and could leave you behind or pull you so fast that you would be floating horizontally to the bike, grabbing the handlebars for all you were worth with your legs trailing behind. Control was needed. Driving fast but being in full control of the bike whilst doing it, and not it being in control of you! A phrase often used was 'Any fool can drive fast enough to be dangerous!'

The techniques I was to learn were based on a combination of *The Advanced Motorist* together with Formula 1. Legal racetrack driving on the open road. Safe and legal! How to overtake. Points of acceleration, etc. I had a slight advantage at the beginning, having been on the Velocette course meant the one handed, standing on the seat, sitting backwards and any other sadistic methods the instructors gave you of learning control/balance was old hat! The only problem was 650 cc and not 200 cc meant that the throttle was a little (no, a lot) more sensitive. Technically, the twist through 45ish degrees meant 0–40 mph on the Velocette but 0–110 mph on the Triumph (dependent upon how well serviced the bike was). It took some getting used to, but 'getting used to' happened and we were soon out onto the open road.

My first instructor was over six-foot-two, probably over seventeen to eighteen stone and had a black beard to die for! Must have been nine inches long! The Mad Monk. Terrific bloke and a great instructor. Well named as I was to find out later but, in the meantime, let's call him Dave.

We were placed in groups of three, our group was under the tutelage of Dave. First thing was coffee—most important—and as we sat round gleaning what was to be expected of us over the next month, Dave found out more about us. Backgrounds, experience in the job, on bikes, all the things necessary for him to know where to pitch the start point.

The first guy had five to six years' service and rode a Honda 50 to and from work. Then there was me with two and a half years' service, plus a 'Noddy' course (as the Velocette course was lovingly called), and riding a Lambretta to and from work. And then there was the third guy! I suppose you get them in all walks of life—the 'been there, done that, got the t-shirt' type. Six to eight years' service, rode a Kawasaki 900, could strip it down and rebuild it in twenty minutes, and riden it all over the world! I'm sure you're getting the picture. There was nothing he had to learn, and he wanted the instructor to know he only needed to teach the two sprogs—*he* didn't need it, but he'd help where necessary! Red rag to the Mad Monk, but not a flicker showed on his face.

We set off for a morning's ride with the Honda 50 owner going first. The instructor would follow, and the two other students would follow him. Instruction was normally in twenty to thirty-minute bites, but this first one was painful for the Kawasaki 900 man! He was champing at the bit to show what he was made of.

We would stop when or if the instructor needed to pass on information to the student under direct tutorship, or to change over.

The second to be tutored was Mr Kawasaki. Dave had hardly finished his instructions before Mr K roared off in a cloud of dust and exhaust. We were a little shocked, but Dave casually turned to

us and said, 'About four or five miles down the road there's a turning
to Hatfield. Take it. We'll be a little way down that road.' And with
that he too roared off—but smoothly, no exhaust clouds, no dust,
just class.

We followed, but soon lost them both in the distance. As Dave had
said, some four to five miles down the road we found the turning to
Hatfield. We took it and, sure enough, hardly a mile down the road
on a right-hand bend we found them. Dave was standing beside his
parked Triumph, whilst Mr K. was struggling to extricate himself
from beneath his!

Apparently, the bend was quite notorious for bikers failing to read
it correctly and coming to grief! The bend wound up on itself and
was liberally covered with loose chippings. None of it conducive to
speed on two wheels—as Mr Kawasaki had found out to his peril.

Dave waited until we'd all parked our bikes and then said to a very
sheepish looking pupil, 'Coffees are on you for the rest of the day, as
is the cleaning of all four bikes when we return. Remember,'—and
then came that quote that I was hearing for the first time and would
never forget—'any fool can ride fast enough to be dangerous!'

Lessons learned all round, particularly by Mr K, who, funnily
enough, became a much more receptive student.

Road work was fantastic. Long trips, short trips. It was nothing
to get on our bikes at around 9.00 am and be back around 5.00 pm
having been to Wales, Wiltshire, West Yorkshire, Cornwall, Cumbria,
or Kent . . . and never have seen a motorway. Short trips were normally
round the Home Counties—but the mileage would be identical.

There was no doubt about it, taking note of everything we were
taught, made for a wonderful riding experience. Man and machine
in perfect harmony, gliding over the road surface like a skater on ice,
swaying as one with corners and hills, road surface changes taken in
stride without missing a beat . . . ah, yes . . . wonderful days.

And then came offroading! Very exciting, very frightening, very exhilarating, very everything a young bloke could wish for. First lesson: 'Any fool can ride fast enough to be dangerous'. Second lesson: 'Be prepared for the unexpected!'

Many years ago, there was a public announcement advertisement about being prepared for the unexpected when driving in fog. What to do and how to do it. A family were driving along a motorway when suddenly the fog fell. What to do? Slow down. Fog lights on. Allow more distance from the vehicle in front, etc. All adhered to by the conscientious, advertisement, driver dad, when out of the fog loomed a heard of elephants! Definitely unexpected on a British motorway! Point made—up came the caption: 'Be prepared . . .'

We weren't expecting elephants, it was a lovely day, no sign of fog, perfect road-riding conditions. We assumed therefore that the conditions off road would be perfect too. Not so. Third lesson: 'Never assume anything!' Regardless! Always watch out for elephants! Just wish I'd remembered.

The bikes were still 650 Triumphs, with all the power of their road brothers, they'd just been adapted for off road riding by changing the forks, tyres, suspension, and so on. They didn't actually do anything a smaller trail bike could do, other than supply more power to the rear wheel. Of course, they were also definitely much heavier!

The Mad Monk got the whole squad to line up facing across an open field. 'See the crown of that oak tree?' Two to three hundred yards in the distance, we could all see the dome of a lonesome oak tree showing just above the brow of a hill. 'When I say go, I want you to race out, round that oak, and back here. The last one back buys the coffee!'

On his command, we, to a man, dropped our heads, pulled the clutch lever in, kicked the bikes into first gear and started to rev the guts from the machine in anticipation of—'Go!'

Brands Hatch had nothing on us. Clutches slipped. Handful of throttle. Clouds of exhaust fumes, mud, stones, and ripped out grass were left floating in the air as twelve tight, I'm-not-buying-the-coffee, rookie would-be-traffic-patrol-officers roared off towards the distant oak.

The guy beside me had gained better purchase on the grass than most of us, and had a slight lead, but there wasn't a gnat's whisker between us as we careened across the field.

It was incredibly exciting to have the freedom of open space, no traffic, and lots and lots of power between our legs as we approached the brow of the hill. Slowly the whole tree began to take shape. Firstly, the lower branches of the tree, then the trunk and finally the grass through which it grew.

As we soared over the hilltop, we were able to take in the entire vista. The one hundredish yards of grass, plus . . . the twentyish yards of mud and watery slime between the hill and the grass!

We were all some three to four feet in the air, almost in a line, and all realising there was absolutely nothing we could do to avoid catastrophe!

We landed axle deep in the mire.

Some of the Metropolitan police would-be-traffic-cops' finest went over their handlebars, some slid serenely to the side, and others, attempting to leave the bikes before they landed, simply ended up face first in the clart (wonderfully descriptive Cumbrian word for slimy mud!). None of us escaped. Bikes, uniforms, bodies—covered from head to foot in clart!

Slowly we extricated ourselves and found the instructors, standing atop the brow in various ecstatic positions of utter glee-cum-euphoria.

Nothing needed to be said, and definitely nothing about elephants was uttered!

There was no doubt about it, we were entering an extremely steep learning curve. This was just the beginning.

The next day we were to learn the basics of off-road biking. Firstly, the nursery slopes, how to negotiate the surprises of off-roading. Something simple before the real slopes were attempted. All of us were still feeling a little raw (and sore!) from the previous day's muddy escapade and were looking forward to being gently introduced to this new world.

In the back of my mind I could hear a little voice saying 'Watch out for elephants! Watch out for elephants! Are these instructors really instructors or are they actually arch-fiendish, bestial monsters from beyond Thunderdome? If the latter ... *watch out*!'

'The latter. Definitely the latter,' I thought as I disappeared over a cliff! Well not really a cliff! It just felt like one. Why? The nursery slope began its journey innocuously enough along a dirt track about ten foot by one foot, through a bramble hedge and onto the track continuation for another five to ten feet before going over 'the cliff'.

There was approximately a twenty-foot gap between riders (i.e. six meters?) not enough to be able to stop and examine 'the cliff' anyway. It was vertical for about a foot—not much I hear you say—before landing on the track again, which was the beginning of the decent at around 1:3 (i.e. for every one foot forward, you drop three). Yes, steep. Very steep. To give the instructors their due, they did tell us, 'On the downhill stretches never touch the clutch'.

'Never touch the clutch!' I thought my time had come as I gazed down this precipice. Not just straight down, but bends, hairpins, and ninety degree turns for around fifty to one hundred feet. On my first decent, I really didn't have time to think about clutch, brakes, throttle, point, nothing except hanging on for grim death until the nightmare was over and I reached the bottom and solace. But solace was brief, very brief ...

At the bottom was a tree round which we turned a hairpin to be faced with the upward track, even steeper, if that was possible, than the downhill section. Still only around a foot wide but strewn with rocks and boulders, and what goes down, must go up (same distance)!

There was ample power in these machines to negotiate such a hill, even pulling my thirteen stone but, again, it was almost a matter of shutting my eyes and going for it. I didn't literally shut my eyes, just my metaphorical ones.

More bends, more hairpins, and then suddenly *Pop!* we emerged back through the bramble hedge, back onto the short track section and level ground.

I was still in one piece and as I prepared to stop the bike, I was met by the gently caressing voice of the instructor, 'What you stopped for? Keep going!'

Couldn't argue with such gentle persuasion and off I set again, back round the nursery slope. When had my trousers got so wet? It wasn't raining! After half a dozen trips round the 'block' I must admit I started thinking 'piece of cake'.

Down and up. Up and down. Wiggle, wiggle. Negotiate bend, rock, dislodged branch. No doubt about it, I had it cracked! But . . .

Fourth lesson: never become blasé!

I was going up for maybe the sixth or seventh time when the rider in front of me grabbed too much throttle, causing his back end to snake. He rectified it, but not before he had dislodged a boulder some foot in diameter and thrown right into the middle of my track. Nowhere to go. Couldn't stop. Couldn't go back. How could I go forward?

I closed my eyes and slithered to the left between boulder and tree, but in so doing lost my rear wheel traction.

The engine screamed and the rear wheel spun freely. Only for a millisecond, but enough to cause my control to be thoroughly impeded. As it landed, so it bit, throwing me backwards. I grabbed the handlebars tightly but in so doing twisted full lock on the throttle.

This was when I realised 650 cc bikes have a lot of power! Before I could shut down the throttle, the bike shot me to the top of the hill and through the bramble hedge like a demented camel with a wasp chewing its backside!

I was airborne and landed inches from the bike in front. Fortunately, I'd had the forethought, somehow, to shut off my revs, but on landing, I was once again thrown backwards on my seat, again causing me to grab a handful of throttle!

Immediately the tyre bit and shot me across the waiting area, causing riders and instructors to scatter.

It's important to note that the waiting area was the top of a hill, around twenty to thirty feet in diameter surrounded by trees and sheer drops on all sides.

I was doing a wheelie at this point, and not, fortunately, still airborne, or I really would have shot into the 'far blue yonder'. Instead it meant that the back wheel struck one of the railway sleepers around the periphery, situated I'm sure for such an occasion (i.e. stopping a demented camel from kamikazeing over the precipice!).

Fortunately, I had parted company with the bike at this stage and was flat on my back staring at the sky, while my bike balanced precariously on the railway sleeper.

The sky suddenly darkened overhead as a beard-clad face stared down at me. 'You okay?' I was about to say 'I think so' when a boot caught me in the ribs and the voice boomed, 'Look at my bike! Look at the state of your uniform!'

I remember thinking about elephants . . . and that fourth rule 'Don't get blasé'!

Chapter Sixteen
General Patrol

Eventually, all good things must come to an end and some weeks later, twelve very happy, very tired, very sore, but very much wiser motorcyclists received there certificates.

I was now a fully-fledged class 3 motorcyclist. No longer only allowed to ride just the Velocettes, but out with the big boys' toys—the Triumph TR6s! 650 cc twins. The Saint.

I suppose today, modern riders would find them hard work, heavy, lacking in power, cumbersome, but to me, back in the '70s, it was a true dream machine.

Class personified. Personally, I still think of them 'class personified' when I see one pass me in the street (and here I give a huge thank you to all you enthusiasts who are searching out, rebuilding, looking after and generally protecting such works of art for future generations—fantastic job) but then maybe I'm remembering through rose-tinted specs! Or am I? Marlon Brando straddled his own Thunderbird 650 cc in *The Wild One*, Elvis Presley, Clint Eastwood, and Bob Dylan all road Bonneville's; Evel Knievel flew one over Caesar's Palace . . . Couldn't have been all bad.

However, that's enough nostalgia for one book!

To be off my 'beat' feet at last and have such a wonderful piece of kit throbbing underneath me was an amazing feeling. Man and machine floating as one round the streets of London.

Of course, it wasn't all 'Look at me. Look at my machine. 'Aren't

I wonderful!' (Many people saw me as just another 'Black Rat' anyway!) Things were to change. It wasn't long before I was cut down to size—and who did I think I was anyway?

It was a beautiful afternoon, and my buddy Bob Sullivan was off duty. I was on my own to 'poodle' around and thought I might take a look in the parks; enjoy the flowers, grass, scenery in general (secretaries and typists on their lunch break didn't come into it, of course, far too busy), when I heard, rather than saw, a moped farther up the road.

The rider didn't appear more than twelve or thirteen. Black smoke was pouring out of the non-existent exhaust pipe, and it wasn't showing any number plates. The young lad had his non-helmeted head down, backside up and going for it, full pelt. He must have been doing at least 25 mph!

I pulled alongside him and signalled for him to pull in. I might as well have been talking to the moon. He didn't even glance in my direction. Head stayed down, staring straight ahead, and twisting full throttle. I tried several times to get his attention to no avail.

What was I to do? I pulled in behind him to contemplate, when suddenly he turned left down a no entry, a one-way-only street. Cars were parked on both sides; fortunately, nothing was coming.

I knew the area and literally a stone's throw farther on was a parallel street leading to the road at the bottom to which he was heading. Rather than follow him down the one way, I took the next street—well he wasn't going to get away from a 650 was he? At the bottom, no moped was in sight and I assumed he simply hadn't got there yet. I turned to meet him, but as I arrived at the other end of the one-way street, I saw him. He'd turned back towards the main road and was now turning left; I should have realised at that point he was streetwise, very streetwise! I raced up the street, and there he was, still head down, bottom up, fifty yards on. I followed, and again pulled alongside him. This time he looked at me, smiled, and rode on!

I thought, 'He's going to hurt himself or someone else if I can't get him stopped,' at which point we entered a roundabout.

Instead of turning left with the not-too-light traffic flow, he turned right! Several cars swerved to miss him but, quite oblivious, he carried on and turned right down the next street off the roundabout.

I thought 'This is crazy' as other motorists pointed in his direction or shouted at me to stop him! (What did they think I was trying to do?!) By the time I got to his turning, going the right way round the round-a-bout, he was again fifty yards ahead of me.

I saw a lady with a pram step in front of him and jump back quicker than she'd stepped out! His riding became more and more erratic, as he ignored traffic lights, pedestrian crossings; he must have broken every law in the book, and I was thinking 'I'll be writing for a week'—if I ever caught him!

That was when he turned down a culvert that I knew led to some waste ground. 'I've got him,' I thought. 'He's going to decamp and run for it.' No such luck. He carried on roaring (at 25 mph!) across the wasteland towards another culvert that led back out onto the road.

I realised I couldn't allow him to do that and made up my mind to 'gently ease him from his machine.' I'd seen plenty of cowboys grab distressed ladies from runaway horses and pull them onto their steeds. How difficult could it be? Trouble was, he wasn't a lady in distress, and this was no runaway horse! This was a little whotsit with no regard for anybody or anything.

My problem has always been thinking too long by which time he'd reached the lane and I'd missed my chance. I entered the lane only feet behind him. Again, all I could do was follow.

I was thinking, 'If I just nudge his back wheel . . . it may be enough to unsteady him, at which time he'll fall off, or at the very least know I'm serious and stop,' when I realised that the lane was getting narrower! The walls began to crowd me, or my bike started getting wider! Seconds later there was a sickening screech of metal as my leg shields met the wall—on both sides! I ground to a halt. Stuck. Handle bars and leg shields completely jammed!

Ten yards on the whotsit stopped, got off, turned round, and waved. Then he got back on his machine and rode off!

I had to look on the bright side, at least I managed to get him to stop! I also think it was quite fortunate I hadn't radioed in for help . . . How would I have explained a 50 cc moped getting away from a 650 cc?

Definitely brought me down a peg or two. Many pegs! (Now there's only you and I that know about it.)

Chapter Seventeen
Chases (or Rather Pursuits)

I did eventually extricate myself from the alley. Very slight grazing to the leg shields, so no real damage done . . . except to my pride! As I've said before, you can be the greatest driver in the world, but you never know what the other bloke is going to do!

I was out with another motorcyclist colleague one damp afternoon in north London when I remember pulling away from a traffic junction and turning left off the main road into a side street, fortunately, as it was to turn out, fairly wide.

We were simply cruising, not going anywhere particular, just waiting for that 'gut' feeling to stir and I was slowly increasing my speed when I saw a car pull out from a turning to my right. He had his left-hand indicator flashing and, assuming he was turning left, I thought no more about it. Except he didn't turn left; he turned right. Right into my path.

I successfully swerved to avoid him and noticed there was a turning to the left only feet away. Still with his left-hand indicator flashing, I thought 'puddin'' and assumed he'd simply turned it on too soon and was intending to turn left there.

Nope! He turned right again. Still flashing left! This time I couldn't avoid a catastrophe. I had nowhere to go and fell off in an unceremonious heap in the middle of the road.

The driver pulled up against the right kerb, beside a post box, got out and posted a letter.

I was 'quite cross' and can remembering picking up my 8 cwt, machine and wanting to throw it at him.

Fortunately, my mate rode up alongside and calmly said, 'Steady, JT. No harm done. One hundred per cent his fault. You have witnesses. Let me deal.'

Thanks to his cool head, he got a statement from a very apologetic driver who said 'I'm so sorry. I didn't see the policeman. My windows were all misted up.'

Later that day, whilst writing up our report, I felt my arm and neck start to stiffen . . . so began a twelve-month period of inactivity. Six months off work followed by six months' light duties. The doctors never did really ascertain what I'd done, but I've had a stiff neck ever since.

* * *

As exciting and exhilarating as big motor cycles were, I must admit that underneath, I preferred a wheel on each corner. Much more stable and certainly drier, warmer, and more comfortable. I suppose I was just a little *nesh* (another good old Cumbrian word for soft, delicate, feeble! I didn't shout it about too much, but I did, and still do, like my home comforts!) All that is to say that as much as I loved the Triumph, big cars are much nicer—and they did get me out of that ✗✳❨☂ Gaberdine nappy!

So Hendon called again. By now, I had done a fair stint on solos, and it was now the right time to go for my advanced car course.

I'd already achieved my class three licence whilst at Costner Street, and that had enabled me to not only drive the pandas but also the vans and plain clothes, unmarked CID cars.

The advanced course was the final step in driving. Pass this course and you were amongst the elite of drivers. A class one or two could be gained, both of which would enable the driver to drive the fast response cars out on division, and cars in general in Traffic.

An amazing course, but definitely not for the faint-hearted. This was when one learnt to drive at speed, safely and well. Here I must pay homage to the driving instructors who had to get the drivers up to the required standard and beyond simply by sitting next to them. Having no control over the car, and yet ever pushing the driver. They must have had nerves of steel!

Hendon instructors were extensively trained themselves and were selected for their ability to read driving situations confidently and cautiously, assess potential driver anxiety, promote safe and defensive driving skills, and yet still make it enjoyable.

Teaching new drivers of whatever level would be hectic, taxing, but no doubt rewarding. The ability of a driving instructor to remain professional, calm, and patient in a stressful situation would in turn help their student remain calm. This would provide an environment that focused on driving proficiency and learning, rather than the nervousness or chaos of the situation.

As students we all made mistakes just like every other driver on the road, and we didn't always learn applicable defensive driving skills or manoeuvres on our first try—practice makes perfect. Our instructors had to be willing to be patient and allow us to make mistakes thereby ensuring we would be able to learn from them, mastering our skills as time progressed.

Instructors who are willing to try different teaching techniques like verbalizing directions, giving physical demonstrations, or drawing out a driving manoeuvre can be beneficial. Students who were having difficulty mastering a skill, or those who learnt differently, required a different approach than other students.

To me, this adaptability while teaching was a key quality of an effective driving instructor because it allowed for a spontaneous pliability that benefited a larger number of students, not simply one group who learnt a specific way. I believe this adaptability was a great tool for finding ways to communicate with everyone.

The Mad Monk was a prime example of this in that many may have thought his techniques unorthodox to say the least, but here I am fifty years on still remembering virtually everything he taught me. His ability to motivate his students through his 'active and engaging training' ensured a successful and productive training session and course.

Driving is a privilege, and not a right and a driving instructor who can proactively bridge the gap between fun and work is an instructor who can communicate the importance of the rules of the road whilst still enjoying the drive. I was blessed with first class instructors throughout my driving career and want to say a huge well done to all instructors out there. I know you can't be responsible for how your student will progress after your work is done, but if quality seeds are planted at the training stage, then one would hope that quality drivers will result.

And so, after an intensive four-week course, I emerged with my class one. I still rode the solos, but once I'd achieved my certificate for cars, I tended to drive them more than the bike. The job was identical except that on the bikes, dealing with congestion was more prevalent. It was much easier and quicker to get to the source of the problem. The cars carried equipment for use at accidents or incidents and the like, and were obviously much more likely to be called to those. However, whatever mode of transport I was allotted too, I still kept that eagle eye for defective or dangerous vehicles and drivers.

And so it was, that one warm, spring Sunday afternoon, I found myself driving a Rover 3500 with Bob as my observer and

R/T operator around the South London area of Kennington. We had the windows open. The smell of warm grass, spring flowers and trees was filling the car when, suddenly, that soporific magic that springtime brings with all its promise for the year ahead was shattered as an ancient Ford Zodiac pulled out of a turning in front of us with copious amounts of obnoxious effluvium (better known as exhaust fumes!) belching out from under, around, and out of the exhaust pipe. We rapidly closed the windows of our car to avoid being asphyxiated.

Bob and I looked at each and, without a word, realised that this vehicle was destined for a stop. I flashed the Rover headlights. Bob tweaked the siren at the same time as giving the blue light a quick burst. One would have thought that the headlights, siren, and blue light together with the Rover being a fully-marked police car would be sufficient for any driver to realise we were a police car wanting a word? Not on your life!

Not only did the Zodiac driver fail to stop but he attempted to accelerate away. The vehicle had already had somewhat of a hard life and an insult like the driver's heavy right foot caused it to cough, spew more black filth into the atmosphere, and then slowly attempt to increase its speed! The poor thing really was tired, and the passengers would have had more success getting away on foot than in that car!

But they persevered; so did we. I've said it before, police vehicles don't chase, they pursue. That means we simply sat on their tail and waited for them to run out of petrol or stop of their own volition—or something! At least that was how we did it then. I watched a traffic cops programme on TV last night and they were using a thing called TPAC which meant that they trebled up the cars and stopped a vehicle by one car going in front of the driver, another close up the rear of the same car, and the third pulling alongside to gradually bring the offender to a halt. It looks amazing when done properly, an incredibly skilful action by highly trained officers, but last night the offending driver just didn't want to be stopped and used his car like a dodgem car—driving into the police cars, backing into them, going up the pavement/grass verge, etc., etc.! I'd never seen anything like it! They eventually got him stopped and arrested but not before he'd written off four (*yes*, four) police cars!

Bob's and my pursuit was like waiting for paint to dry compared to that! Slowly their speed increased until around 40–45 mph was reached! They obviously dared not stop for fear of ever getting started again. Hence red lights, pedestrian crossings, and stop signs were all ignored.

We called into Scotland Yard communications for a vehicle check and found it of no interest to the police but owned by a female. There was a female in the passenger seat, but the driver had a beard!

I doubt if I'd be exaggerating to say that almost every street in SE London was covered, well, almost, but it was twenty-five minutes later that we approached the Elephant and Castle.

In those days, the road system at the Elephant was made up of two roundabouts joined by a 100 yards of dual carriageway, and regardless of what speed one was travelling, 40–45 mph was too fast to negotiate the hazard!

Our bearded friend, however, neither slowed nor deviated, but hit the first roundabout in a cloud of exhaust fumes narrowly missing a London Transport bus already in the system. Our driver swerved, skidded, and fought to gain control of his car, but at 40–45 mph 100 yards is soon traversed.

The second roundabout loomed. Having gained a modicum of control, but failing to lose any speed, he entered. Fortunately, being a

Sunday afternoon, traffic was light. The bus driver, already in a state of shock, saw what was happening and hung back. So did we as we watched the drama unfold!

Only just having gained control from the first roundabout, the driver now totally lost it. The car swung to its left, then right, and then tipped onto its offside as it began to somersault. Firstly onto its roof, then its nearside and back onto its wheels. As it toppled onto its offside yet again, so the driver's door was flung open, throwing the driver out and into the air. He was like a rag doll—all arms and legs. He must have travelled fifteen feet into the air before landing flat on his back in the middle of the road. He didn't move as the vehicle continued its dizzying dance, finally coming to rest on its roof.

Seeing the driver still, totally inert, not going anywhere in a hurry, and anticipating the car could burst into flames at any moment, we decided to check on the other passenger we'd seen in the car. Save at least one life—hopefully. At first, we could see no one in the car and then, a frail voice from the rear mewed, 'I'm stuck.'

Slowly we saw a young woman of around twenty scrambling from the rear seats to the front and then out of the window. Amazingly, she appeared to be unharmed. Seeing she was okay, I left her with Bob and went to see how the driver was faring.

Nobody was in the road! I looked all around. Nobody! I asked the bus driver if he'd seen where the driver had gone, but he'd been watching us and seen nothing. I was totally confused! I'd been expecting to see a broken body, and to find nothing . . . I returned to Bob who was looking equally confused. 'The driver's gone,' I said bewilderedly.

'I know,' said Bob. 'And she says she was driving the car alone! She says it's hers and that she's a learner driver. That's why she didn't stop. She knew she should have a full licence holder with her and she was frightened!'

We questioned the bus driver, but he hadn't seen anything. Not even the driver flying in the air! A small crowd had gathered, but no-one had seen anything of the driver or even seen anyone lying in the road! The girl stuck to her story and the driver never did come to light.

To this day Bob and I know what we saw, but . . . ?

* * *

Have you ever noticed how minute events in your life can have major impacts upon your life? For example, you can't find your wallet. You spend an extra five minutes looking for it and miss the bus. On the next bus you meet a girl who ends up being your wife!

It's the *Sliding Doors* film for real.

What if I'd become a doctor instead of a policeman? What if I'd stayed in Carlisle and never gone to London? What if . . . ? What if . . . ? My life would have gone down a totally different route. I'd not have met my amazing wife! I'd not have had my terrific kids! How different would my life have been? It could certainly not have been any better. I'm so grateful I took the left fork and not the right way back when. I'm a very happy and contented man.

Such a 'Y' junction instance took place shortly after our first son was born. He would have been around twelve to eighteen months old and crawling. Giving him a quick cuddle and toss in the air, followed by a quick cuddle with my wife—no toss in the air, I hasten to add—I left for work on my gleaming Honda 70 cc motorcycle.

I was posted to a solo motorcycle that day. Nothing different to any other day except that on the way out, I happened to notice a forensic science book that had been left out, open at a page depicting a sixteen- to eighteen-month-old toddler grasping the central bar of an electric fire. The fire was on. Forensic science books, by their very nature, contain material to turn the strongest stomachs. Pictures of murders, suicides, accidents . . . All necessary, of course, for those studying that particular career or vocation route.

The simplest definition of forensic science according to most dictionaries is:

> Any science used within the criminal justice system. While this definition may be simple, the field of forensic science is anything but simple. Crime scene investigators and lab technicians use specialized skills and tools to collect, analyse, and present evidence in order to solve a crime or successfully convict the offender.

In training we had been told we needed to see this type of book to know what our forensic specialists did, how they could help us and 'to toughen us up!' I'd rather not have been 'toughened up' but, looking back through my career, I can see the necessity of it . . . I didn't like it though!

Suffice to say that one of these books had been left in the office, open at this particular page. I couldn't get the image out of my mind. All day, all I could see was my Carl grasping a hot electrical element. I rang Ange to ensure she'd guarded the fire and was keeping our son away from it. In the end I had to take time off. I just couldn't concentrate.

My little Honda was hot when I got home. Very hot. I can remember running in and shouting, 'Is everything all right? Is the fire on? Is it guarded?'

Ange must have thought I'd taken leave of my senses. Carl was in the middle of the room and crawling towards me. I picked him up and almost crushed the life out of him as I buried my face in his little woolly, baby-smelling jumper and inwardly wept in my exuberance at seeing him okay.

It was only a couple of days later when, once again, he was crawling around on the floor. He was heading for the fire. Stretching a little podgy hand out towards the glowing red middle bar. The forensic image blasted a hole in my brain. I can remember shouting and throwing my paper in the air as I jumped up to grab him.

'No! No!' I screamed and pulled him back. I hit his little hand, quite hard. Much harder than I intended 'Hot! Hot! Hot!' I can see those little shocked eyes staring at me, slowly filling with tears as the pain of my slap mixed with, 'What is my daddy doing?' reached his little brain.

He's mid forties now and, without doubt, my best mate. If I've asked his forgiveness once for hitting him so hard, I've asked a hundred times, and each time he's put his arms round me and said, 'But you loved me, Dad!'

Today he has children of his own and knows exactly how I felt. The vision of that forensic photograph, and those big tear-filled eyes has never left me. Did I change Carl's life that day? Would things have turned out differently if I hadn't overreacted? Did I overreact? Would things have been different if I'd not seen the forensic book? I suppose we'll never know, but at least my son is six foot today and a man of whom I am very proud . . . with two very healthy hands.

Chapter Eighteen
Careful Who You Work With!

In all walks of life there are personality conflicts. The police force is no exception. Sometimes you just never see eye to eye with someone and they never see eye to eye with you. Everybody else gets on fine with them. It's just you that has a difficulty. And vice versa! Then there's the time you see someone else not getting on with someone else and vice versa, but you do! You know what I mean! Personality conflicts.

Of course there are people that no one gets on with nor do they get on with anyone else. There was such a guy on my shift: Dom.

I tried my hardest to get on with him. Didn't work. No matter what I did, it didn't make any difference. In the end it hurts when you bang your head against a wall, and it's better to stop before you make it bleed!

However, there were times when I just couldn't avoid being double-manned with him in the car. It wasn't just the personality conflict that bothered me, but the way things boiled out of him on members of the public that worried me more. I used to feel that I would get sucked into problems of his making.

One particular peaceful, spring Sunday morning, I'd been so double crewed. He was driving and I was the passenger when, on the New Kent Road flyover, we were passed by a Rover 2000. 'Look at that ✗✶✦✦! What a ✗✶✦✦ I'm going to ✗✶✦✦ him!'

I nearly jumped out of my skin! I think I was dropping off and beginning to think Dom had too as he had been doing somewhere in the region of 20 mph since leaving the Elephant and Castle. The sudden expletives frightened the life out of me.

Conversation, as some might term it with Dom, had been good. I suppose I'd been lulled into a false sense of security with the peaceful, innocuous nature of the general chat. And then—All hell broke loose.

He floored our Rover. Three and a half thousand cc of unleashed power kicking in. Literature stated 0–60 in a little over nine seconds. Fast for its day . . . but they lied. As my face pealed back like the skin on a boiled tomato, I was certain they'd lied. We were just coming off the flyover and I thought my time had come as the rear of the 2000 rapidly approached.

I slowly slid down in my seat and Dom screamed across me at the totally bemused gent we were now parallel with. The poor guy's pipe almost fell out of his mouth as his horn-rimmed specs slid down his nose. In a fluster, he pulled onto the side of the road. His manoeuvre impressed me as the obvious thoughts of his Sunday dinner mingled with the steering wheel, brakes, turning, and maniac screaming at him from the ether bombarded his brain.

Dom was out of the car almost before we'd stopped and running back to the bemused driver.

'Who do you think you are? Fangio?' I could hear lilting on the breeze.

What poor Mr Ordinary-Joe-Soap-owner-of-the-Rover must have thought, goodness only knows. Embarrassment didn't come into what I thought, as I remained firmly in my seat. When stopping vehicles, we would normally both have a gut feeling or similar that something wasn't quite right with a vehicle and stick together during the stop; supporting one another should anything go pear-shaped. Hence, I should have got out of the car and checked the driver's tax disc, tyres, general condition of the car, together with control room checks regarding the vehicle and so on while my partner dealt with the driver—but on this occasion—discretion was the better part of valour!

I was fuming. Everything within me wanted to get out and apologise to the accosted gentleman. Eventually Dom returned to the car, 'That'll teach him to drive like a moron!' he said as we pulled away.

'No matter how wrong a person might be, no one deserves to be spoken to like that!' I said. (Put somewhat more politely than it was actually said!) and continued to give him both barrels. I remember finishing by sayin,g 'Now take me back to the garage. I have things to do. And should that gent complain, he has me as his witness.'

Just before I leave Dom . . . I remember being posted one night with him as my regular partner Bob was off. The chat was good and, as usual, we covered most of the topics blokes rabbit about until around 3.00 am when we were cruising one particularly rough area of our ground skirting a canal: Wells Way.

The lighting, what had been left of it, was poor. More empty beer cans and dog 'poppy-poo-pars' than anything else. It's a road one wouldn't walk down in the daylight, let alone at three o'clock in the morning . . . and yet there, walking in the gloom, was a tall, slim figure of what we assumed was a male.

'Bit late to be taking the air, eh?' said Dom to me, as he slowed the vehicle and pulled up alongside the man.

The guy stopped stock still and stared straight ahead as Dom, in his own inimitable way, started his interrogation technique.

'F—in' late ain't it, pal?'

No reply. Not even a flicker from the apparition standing beside Dom's open window.

'I said it's f—in' late, pal. Where you been?'

Still not a word. Not a movement.

I could feel Dom winding up for one of his tirades, so I slithered down in my seat trying to pretend I wasn't there, but at the same time, trying to get a better look at who Dom was speaking to.

He was obviously very tall and slim, but a floppy fedora was pulled forward over his eyes, hiding them, but accentuating his long, beaky nose and chin. Not dissimilar, I thought, to Punch or maybe the Wicked Witch of the West!

'Are you deaf or just plain stupid?' said Dom as he slowly straightened in his seat, and I slid further down.

'This is not good,' I thought to myself and even wished I was back on the street, out in the rain, slowly plodding my beat, with the friendly raindrops caressing the back of my neck. (Shows how bad it was.) Anywhere but here. I noticed the guy had his hand tucked between the buttons of his overcoat, out of sight. Something I noticed Dom was slowly realising.

'What you got in your coat?' Dom asked, lowering his voice a little.

For the first time the guy moved and bending down with the speed of light, he stared, nose to nose, through the window at Dom.

Still he didn't speak.

I'm sure I heard the contents of Dom's stomach being released as he realised—for the first time—that this was no ordinary guy!

With his face only inches from Dom's, he said, 'I gotta knife,' in a quiet, slow drawl, as the beer and tobacco-infested breath surged through the window, engulfing Dom. 'And I'm gonna stick it straight through your heart!'

For the first time in my life I was thankful for headrests. Otherwise I'm sure my neck would have broken with the force with which the Rover surged down the road; Dom's foot flat on the floor!

'You not nicking him then, Dom?' I asked, after I'd managed to peel my lips back off the rest of my face.

'Na. Nutter,' was all he replied and continued to stare resolutely out of the rain-drenched windscreen.

It was the first time I actually felt sorry for Dom. I only had to live with him for those few hours at work—he had to live with himself twenty-four-seven!

I never did find out whether Dom learnt any lessons that day. Never saw the guy again either—nor did he ever make a complaint.

I've always thought of myself as pretty easy going, with not very many people fitting into the 'Dom' category in my life, but when they do, I try to think, 'Where's the attitude coming from? Why are they behaving like that?' I feel that there must be something going on in their lives that causes it. Sounds a bit superiority orientated, doesn't it? Believe me, I'm far from perfect and I'm certainly no psychotherapist but . . . . I remember once getting ready for church when my wife put a pair of shoes on that I didn't like. I thought she knew I didn't like them and was surprised to see them on her feet. A discussion ensued which started off at a pretty low level and went down from there. Ultimately all talk ended, and a steaming 'fug' was left! You could cut the atmosphere with a knife.

It wasn't my fault! She shouldn't have put those shoes on, should she. Should she? Anyway, we were going to church and couldn't sort it out there and then, could we? Could we?

I remember going through the door into the church vestibule to be greeted by a larger-than-life character who gripped my hand and shook it as though he would never see me again. I smiled and attempted to retrieve my hand.

'Wonderful day, brother. Wonderful day. Good to be alive, isn't it?'

I felt like spitting in his eye but instead made some inane comment like 'Absolutely, brother. Wonderful day,' giving him an enormous grin, from which I thought Ange would vomit! Well, I bet his wife had put the right shoes on, hadn't she? Hadn't she?

Amazing how easy it is to put a face on to the world. Here was my wife and I, going into church, lying to everyone by actions, pompously pious, pretending all was well when it quite simply wasn't! On top of which she'd kept the same shoes on!

You might be thinking, 'Where's he going with this?' Well . . . you just never know how the person who's cheesing you off left his or her house that morning. Was that someone in their lives wearing the shoes he or she didn't like?

There are always two sides, or more, to every situation, you're not always right. Nor are they! Even when you know they're wrong!

Dom left the shift shortly after that. I never knew why, but always wished I'd been able to talk with him a bit more. I just wondered how often his wife had worn the wrong shoes?

Chapter Nineteen
It Wasn't All Work, Work, Work

When I say my work was not all work, work, work, I don't mean work in the normal sense of the word *work*, but work in a nice sense; I don't mean work, work, work, work wasn't nice, I just mean working easier work than work, work, work. Do you see what I mean?

Perusing the London parks in spring, summer and autumn for example was very nice work. All sorts of things happen in parks from multifarious misdemeanours to sun bathers! Not that sunbathers were of interest to fit, healthy, red-blooded single males, of course. Their modes of dress (or undress) were interesting though. That was quite nice work.

Another part of the solo rider's tour was that of escort duties. They included everything from blood runs (ensuring blood supplies were transported from A to B as quickly as possible) to ambulance runs (ensuring seriously ill people were transported from wherever to wherever as quickly and smoothly as possible, sometimes ultra-slow and smooth depending upon the condition of the casualty) to large loads getting from A to B. They were both carried out in an identical manner (just at different speeds).

A typical run consisted normally of three solo motorcycles plus the escorted unit. There would be the first and second lead bikes in front of the unit with a 'tail-end-Charley' behind.

The object, as I said, was to ensure that the what or who was escorted with the utmost speed, safety, and smoothness from location to location. The lead bike would go to the first junction (whether covered by automated signals or not) to ensure all traffic stopped. Once the escort was through the junction the second lead would speed on to the next junction and again ensure all traffic had stopped while the tail-end-Charley would overtake the said unit and wait his turn to go to the following junction. Meanwhile the original lead bike would leave his junction, catch up, and become tail-end-Charly, and then at his appointed time would leapfrog the unit and become second lead awaiting his turn to become first lead.

You get the general picture?

The procedure is fine until one starts to negotiate town traffic (particularly London traffic—and even more particularly in rush hour—it leads to some very interesting riding!). For anyone familiar with London traffic, or indeed any town, you will know what I mean!

It becomes even more interesting when the escort is a large load. A large load is defined in road transport as:

> An oversize load (or overweight load) is a load that exceeds the standard or ordinary legal size and/or weight limits for a truck to convey on a specified portion of road, highway or other transport infrastructure, such as air freight or water freight. In Europe it may be referred to as special transport or heavy and oversized transportation. There may be load per axle limits. However, a load that exceeds the per-axle limits, but not the overall weight limits, is considered overweight. Examples of oversize/overweight loads include construction machines (cranes, front loaders, backhoes, tanks, etc.), pre-built homes, containers, construction elements (bridge beams, generators, windmill propellers, rocket stages, industrial equipment).

Basically big brutes. Very big brutes . . .

During my time in London, the Thames Barrier was being

constructed and a lot of the elements required for the build fell within this category and had to be brought from Rainham in Essex. The route, and which Big Brute would take it depended on weight, height, length, etc. As it is such a specific science, we had a group in Scotland Yard whose sole purpose was to work out such routes. Sometimes London bridges, for example, just wouldn't take the weight. Often, bends on normal routes were incapable of being negotiated by long loads, or bridges simply too low to get under.

It was nothing to have a generator weighing up to four hundred tons or a girder over a hundred yards long and maybe twenty-eight feet high. It amazed me that routes were ever found for such loads. Sometimes routes were thought to be okay but, in fact, weren't! Very rarely was this the case as costs for damage to roadside property or goods in transit were exorbitant. Heads rolled on such occasions.

One such load we were to escort was a 'girder-type thing' fifteen-feet-six-inches-high. Now, apparently, when Don-Bur first started doing double decks over thirty years ago, they were commonly built at a maximum of sixteen feet; however, today, that limit is often being tested where the degree of clear space between trailer top and bridge has shrunk to just a few inches. Taking into account 'bump and roll', this can be eaten away to a very slim margin. Our men at the Yard, needless to say, conferred at length with the various companies to ensure every 'i' was dotted, and 't' crossed regarding the heights and widths, etc., of the said loads.

On this occasion , as I said, ours was fifteen-foot-six-inches high. We were just escorts, nothing to do with the decision-making whatsoever; our route-finding boffins at the top had chosen and okayed our route of travel. Our documentation said so! Hence, when we picked up our ninety-seven-foot, thirty-ton, fifteen-foot-six-inches-high 'girder-type thing' we were not concerned so much with its height as its length and ensuring the rear steer-driver was able to negotiate bends. Rear steer was a fascinating science in itself to watch these men at work; the load appearing to go straight on when the cab had long since turned right!

The route we'd been given was approximately thirty miles in duration and consisted mainly of A roads with one section being approximately five miles of dual carriageway. The dual track had only one bridge and no bends.

The load was light (thirty tons for these monster trucks is like a flee on a dog's back) and therefore the dual track was a time for us to get a move on; to make up for time lost when we had had to negotiate bends.

One bridge! The headroom on all bridges is at least five metres (sixteen-foot-six-inches) unless signed. We were fifteen-foot-six . . . No problem.

It was a lovely evening; the traffic was light and we were simply cruising along at around 30 mph. We were commandeering the nearside two lanes of the dual track and could have probably managed with just the nearside one. We were of normal width, but why tempt providence? Two lanes gave us much more room to play with.

I can remember looking back at approaching traffic when suddenly there was an enormous metallic bang, more like an explosion!

The shock almost threw me from my motorcycle in consternation. It was one of those occasions when you feel your life flashing before you as your brain attempts to make sense of what is happening.

Horrendous crashing sound; control of severe wobbling bike; sight of aghast faces of following drivers; looking forward and seeing your mates attempting to correct wobbles on their own bikes as their brains do the tango with yours . . . all in a millisecond.

And then the realisation hits you. The impossible has happened. A ninety-seven-foot, thirty-ton, fifteen-foot-six-inches-high 'girder-type thing' was lodged in a bridge! But it couldn't be, the bridge was higher than our load—our paperwork said so, the boffins said so—it couldn't be! Yet there it was!

Not a word was spoken as we parked our motorcycles and stared at the carnage. The drivers did the same, just accented their looks of horror with some colourful expletives.

Amazingly, the damage wasn't as great as we thought. The girder was almost totally undamaged; the bridge had some bent bits, but all in all we realised how lucky we had been. No-one was hurt. There had been no one on the bridge. Passing traffic had been unaffected and untouched. All that remained was . . . what to do now!

There's little use in explaining this part—boring. Suffice to say that we had a long night with lots of writing, but we were totally exonerated, as were the drivers. Someone's head somewhere no doubt rolled, and someone's cheque book somewhere else ended up a lot lighter!

We never found out why it happened—possibly road repairs had raised the road surface, maybe the tyres had been over inflated— maybe the bump and roll of the vehicle had been contributory—who knows—thankfully, we were all in one piece and I never experienced anything like it again.

So that was work, but not work, work. Far too much fun!

* * *

Probably one of the most colourful, fun-loving, noisy (in a nice way), non-work-work, knees-ups in the UK must be the Notting Hill Carnival.

They were first held in 1966 as an offshoot of the Trinidad Carnival, celebrating Caribbean culture and traditions in London. . . . You can usually expect to see fifty thousand performers in the parade and more than thirty sound systems, with more than one million people attending over the carnival weekend.

Professor David Dabydeen, a Guyanese-born broadcaster, novelist, poet and academic, said:

> Carnival is not alien to British culture. Bartholomew Fair and Southwark Fair in the eighteenth century were moments of great festivity and release. There was juggling, pickpocketing, whoring, drinking, masquerade— people dressed up as the Archbishop of Canterbury and indulging in vulgar acts. It allowed people a space to free-up, but it was banned for moral reasons and for the anti-authoritarian behaviour that went on like stoning of constables.
>
> Carnival allowed people to dramatise their grievances against the authorities on the street . . . Notting Hill Carnival single-handedly revived this tradition and is a great contribution to British cultural life.

Stoning constables! Probably a good job they were banned! Never saw that, thank goodness. (I did see much to make my hair stand on end—well, I was/am a simple Cumbrian bloke after all—but I didn't see quite the throwback to the eighteenth century that the professor described.) However, in the main, it was an extremely joyous and fun time that everybody seemed to enjoy to the full.

I suppose the only snag was/is that this type of occasion seemed to attract the—how can I put it—the loutish section of society. You know, the so-called 'football fans' that love to fight, throw bottles at opposing fans, get jugged up until they can't stand, and generally cause as much mayhem as possible . . . nothing to do with football fans at all! Or the peaceful marches that start off fine and then turn sour! Nothing to do with those that have a genuine mission—it's simply the louts that enjoy getting off on spoiling others' enjoyment.

What do they enjoy about spoiling others fun and causing

trouble anyway? After arresting a few and asking them, 'Why are you doing this? What's the point?'

The only answer I got was, 'Dunno!' or 'It's a laugh, eh?' or 'Everybody else was doing it!'

I'm sure psychiatrists out there, and people who are much more learned than I am, will tell us the 'why', but get far enough back in their history and inevitably you'll find a lack of parenting (particularly fathering), being misunderstood as children for a variety of reasons, bullying, lovelessness, etc. Anyway, these people are one of the reasons we are called to such events; to remove them and to ensure that everyone else has a good time.

My main role as a traffic officer at such events was traffic flow— but as Notting Hill is completely blocked (in its entirety), there wasn't a lot for me to do!

Normally I ended up with the Metrolux lighting. At the time this was an extremely high-powered lighting system, which we connected to the police Land Rover, normally for use at accidents, various incidents, and the like. But again, the carnival was already wonderfully lit, so there was little use for the Metrolux either. In the several years that I attended the festivities as Metrolux officer I never used it! So . . . What to do? Cards? Football? Engagement with the fun? As I said in the title of this chapter, it wasn't all work, work, work!

In the main, policemen and carnivalists mingled wonderfully. It was a time of real connectedness with the public. In one small window, people saw policemen as people and not just a uniform. I remember great times and a definite sense of togetherness with the community. Unfortunately, engagement with the public is, today, dare I say, woefully missing. It seems the only time the general public mixes with a policeman is in times of trouble or stress.

Later in my career, I was to work in a department called

Community Affairs (later called Community Relations). Why we stopped having affairs and started relationships, I don't know!

My role then was as the force exhibitions officer. I was responsible for designing and setting up exhibitions throughout the force area, showing the wider aspects of policing from crime prevention through to CID, underwater units and dogs, to communications and forensics.

For many years we used to exhibit in a hundred-foot square marquee at the Three Counties Showground in Malvern, with water wheels and fountains in the centre—flowers and water falls at every turn—and background music playing. Jacob sheep proudly on display, climbing walls for the kids, graffiti walls on which to doodle, and paper hats and badges to put on mums and dads by their offspring.

Whatever did that have to do with policing, I hear you say? Well, not a lot in one sense, but what it did do was to show the public that policemen had noses on their faces and didn't just carry speed cameras! That we could laugh and cry just like they did. Ordinary people with ordinary lives, just like them, with homes, wives, and children.

Our department really connected with the public in those days. For one thing, the children weren't afraid to come and talk to us. When I was on the street, I used to have quite strong words with mums who would say to a crying juvenile, 'Look, there's a policeman. I'll get him to take you away if you don't stop crying!' What a thing to say! How could we get children to come to us when they were in trouble or needed advice if parents were scaring the life out of them with talk like that!

At our shows and exhibitions we used to lark about with them and I had a great time with them and their parents, yet at the same time got the then message over to them: 'Don't talk to strangers!' for the kids and 'Lock it or lose it!' for mums and dads.

I remember at one show having a fish pond as the central exhibit, with goldfish swimming around in it, when two of my colleagues, Mick Franz-Sergeant and Jack Hince, got on their knees beside the pool, gathered a number of children around them, and carried out the perfect candid camera sketch!

Jack said, 'Which one do you like, Mick?'

'I think I like that one,' says Mick.

'So do I,' says Jack and slapped the water, bringing out what looked like a goldfish wiggling between his fingers. Bites it in half and gives the other half to Mick!

There was total silence for a second and then pandemonium let loose as kids shouted, 'Mummy, those policemen just ate a goldfish!'

That drew another crowd who all wanted to see these policemen eating goldfish. Of course, if you ever saw the sketch you'll remember that the wiggling goldfish was, in fact, a sliver of carrot. Needless to say, Jack and Mick were very quick to enlighten the stunned crowd and progress onto showing them how to do it.

What did that have to do with police work? Actually, nothing at all, but the connectedness of policeman and child just couldn't be measured. Those kids thought Jack and Mick were the bees' knees and a pound to a penny, they still remember that incident to this day and hold it with fond memories all these years later.

I've always believed that society can be split roughly into three equal parts. One third pro-police, one third anti-police, and the final third swayed by the media. By that I mean that what many people read in the newspapers, or see on TV, swings them from being pro-police to anti-police at any given moment.

Consider the statement 'Dog Bites Man'. Not terribly news worthy. Unfortunately, it happens all too often and may end up in the fourth column of the fifth page, if at all. Now consider the statement 'Man Bites Dog!' Headlines! Very newsworthy and it will sell lots of newspapers because of its rare occurrence.

Now I know that newspapers have to make a profit—that's the name of the game. They're a business when all is said and done, but sometimes newsworthy items are not always the best news.

'Man Bites Dog' is a great headline and although it's not so good for the dog, would no doubt make a great read. But what about 'Man Bites a Policeman'? Yes, it would no doubt reach the local press—as a headline? Doubtful. Possibly the second or third page? But 'Policeman Bites a Man'. Of course, if the facts are correctly recorded and the policeman *did* bite the man then he has no excuse and deserves all he gets—and then some. Policemen are there to uphold the law, and if there is no justification for hitting (or biting) the said individual then, as I said, they deserve everything they get. The police force wants to get rid of bad or bent coppers as much as anyone. I joined to serve the public, as did 99.9 per cent of my mates, and any one of them would be glad to help turn the key on the cell of a rotten copper!

But sometimes, dare I say, the facts get gilded or omitted to 'make a better story' or photographs get left with no caption for the reader to make up their own mind.

To make my point, and as a quick aside, I won a Mr Universe Competition when I was twelve years old at Butlins, and somehow my local paper got hold of it! Round they came, pens in hand asking loads of questions. I was quite excited to be 'famous' and the centre of attention for once. After they left, we obviously eagerly awaited the paper coming to print. It did! Headline: 'Mammy and Daddy are Proud of their Big Boy!' All the rest of the story was utter twaddle, leaving us wondering who had been interviewed, because it certainly wasn't us! 'John has to take his passport with him every time he travels on the bus'. Absolute nonsense! Gilding the lily?

I suppose no harm was done other than my embarrassment and having a red face at school the next morning.

However, we've no doubt all seen the photographs of policemen with truncheons drawn at demonstrations? Never a mention of why. Was it a bad copper who threw his weight around or was he one that had been on duty for many hours, no break, being pushed and shoved from all angles, abused *ad nauseam*, taunted, threatened, etc., etc.? Any policeman reading this will, as I do, know exactly how it feels with that type of reporting. Rightly or wrongly, truncheons were only supposed to be drawn as a very last resort—but 'Even a worm will turn'!

Did you know that the proverbial saying 'a worm will turn' is first found in John Heywood's 1546 glossary *A Dialogue Conteinyng the Nomber in Effect of All the Prouerbes in the Englishe Tongue*. 'Treade a worme on the tayle, and it must turne agayne.' Neither did I until I looked it up! Shakespeare, never one to avoid borrowing a neat expression, used the same notion a few years later in *Henry VI* part III:

> Who 'scapes the lurking serpents' mortal sting?
> Not he that sets his foot upon her back.
> The smallest worm will turn being trodden on,
> And doves will peck in safeguard of their brood!

Newspapers are amazing pieces of literature, but some editors need to realise that they have the power for evil, as well as good. I remember once doing a talk at a Women's Institute meeting on 'Women's Safety on the Street' shortly after a photograph of an elderly lady had appeared on the front page of a tabloid showing her with a black eye and thick lip with the headline 'Robbed For Her Pension'. Great photograph. Great headline. Many papers sold, but from that one headline thousands of women of all ages were afraid to leave their houses for fear of being attacked! Yet statistically that type of attack is extremely rare. One set of statistics I read said that 1.3 per cent of women were victims of violent crime in the UK for the year ending March 2020 and of those 92 per cent were by people known to them. Of course one crime is one crime too many, and we all know that there are 'lies, damn lies and statistics' but it seems that this type of crime is rare. On that 'Robbed for Her Pension' occasion, was it not possible for the newspaper to be sold on another topic other than one that petrified the life out of our female population?

Sorry, went off on one there! Back to my one third anti-police, one third pro-police and one third swayed by the media. The thing is that the one third pro-police probably will always be, which is great news. Regrettably the one third that are anti-police will also probably always be so. Not good news. But the one third in the middle will sway! So the swaying is very easy depending on the headline, wouldn't it be wonderful for the 'swayed by the media' fraction to be positively swayed rather than negatively?

Of course it's not just the media that needs to 'play the sway!' For example, today more emphasis is probably placed on crime than crime prevention. What do I mean by that? Simply that back in my day, if the CID and Community Affairs departments were vying for money, CID could say 'We arrested one hundred villains last month.' Great news, but the question to us 'How many crimes did you deter?' was unanswerable. How do we know how many crimes were stopped by a policeman simply walking down the street? Or by Mr Bloggs locking his car before going shopping? Or by any number of people simply applying crime prevention measures to property, themselves and so on? These questions just cannot be answered.

'We need value for money!'

'We need results that are quantifiable!'

Regrettably, in a world where figures count, quantifying the result is paramount!

The trouble is I think that the idea of professional policing (which was taken up by Sir Robert Peel when he became home secretary in 1822 and enacted with his Metropolitan Police Act of 1829 establishing a full-time, professional, and centrally organised police force for the greater London area known as the Metropolitan Police) has been somewhat forgotten!

What do I mean and why?

Because the first thing that was ever told to a 'bobby' (so named after their creator, Sir Robert Peel) and the first thing I ever learned in training school (said by his mate Sir Richard Mayne also in 1829) was:

> The primary object of an efficient police force is the prevention of crime. The next that of detection and punishment of offenders if a crime is committed. To these ends all efforts of police must be directed.

Quantifiable versus non-quantifiable?

Yes, we all want to see the villains 'banged up' so we can sleep safer in our beds, but how much better if we started by making things harder for them in the first place!

Just before I leave the point, another example of 'the sway' going the wrong way I suppose could be speed cameras? Somehow, I doubt they engender the same camaraderie with the public that Mick and Jack did with their goldfish and carrot joke? We all know that drivers need to slow down, and that the introduction of cameras has saved many a life, which is wonderful and very much needed, but that isn't my point. Can't we somehow achieve a little balance! CID and Crime Prevention, for example, 'Working together'? Carrots, goldfish, and speed cameras somehow achieving the same goal?

Surely a good police force is a police force that makes a difference together for the people it serves. Maybe courts, government, and newspapers should do the same and say 'We played the sway!' and now two thirds of the public are pro-police!

Chapter Twenty
Noon at the OK Corral
(Tombstone had nothing on S.E. London)

This story, which was to personify the OK Corral, looking back, was probably one of those 'Y' junctions in my life. Or the cause of one anyway. My life was going to be on the line. Things could have gone either way! Fortunately all was well. But what if it hadn't been? What if it had all gone pear-shaped! I had a wife, children, responsibilities . . . it wasn't just me anymore. What if . . . ?

I was getting on a bit. All of thirty-one going on thirty-two! Not that that was the problem, it was the 'only me' bit that changed; I had got married a few years earlier to Angie. Not that that was a problem either, it just meant that my responsibilities had increased. If anything happened to me . . .

She was everything a fellow could ever want; looks, figure, nature (you might think she's hanging over my shoulder as I write) but no—she really was, and still is, great. (Nearly fifty years on from saying 'I do', I still think she's great.)

We'd met on a riverboat party on the Thames. Great party and I was sure we'd clicked. She gave me her name and address and, would you believe it, she was a trainee midwife at the Woolwich Home for Mothers and Babies. Woolwich, London! I lived in Greenwich, London! Just over the hill almost. Perfect.

Except, I didn't get her telephone number. However, just being over the hill meant I could simply pop round and see her. The snag was, I didn't allow for the Gestapo in reception!

I hardly need to describe the 'lady' I met. Half glasses, single, bun on the back of her head, twin set and pearls? Actually . . . nothing like. This one was worse! I'm sure she meant well, and thought she was serving the best interests of the young ladies under her care . . . something like that anyway . . .

'Hello. Is it possible to see Angie, please?'

'Who's Angie?' Her tone should have instantly told me to back off!

'Angie Rowett,' I asked, not realising I'd given the wrong pronunciation to her surname, I mean how many ways can you say it? Whatever, there must have been another way to say it.

'No Angie Rowett here!' and no change in her tone either.

I'd been speaking through a sliding glass hatch—it slammed shut.

I kept my cool. 'I'm sorry,' I mouthed, 'this was the address she gave me.'

She slid the glass back and stared at me for several seconds, then said, 'I don't care what she gave you. There's no one of that name here.' Bang!

I got out my warrant card and again mouthed, 'Look I'm a police officer and I can assure you . . .' On and on I went, but the hatch never opened again!

What do you do? Probably the same as I did unless you had a death wish. I certainly wouldn't have taken her on, not by my lonesome that was for sure! So I did what I reckon many another poor young bloke had done in the past—crept away with my tail between my legs!

It was to be two years before I ever met her again (Angie, not the Gestapo!). I'd never forgotten her. How could you? Several ladies later and none ever coming close. I'd virtually given up.

Believe me I tried all my super-sleuthing tricks to find her, but to no avail. She'd apparently disappeared off the face of the earth.

I was a member of the Christian Police Association in those

days and sang trios with another policeman called Don and his wife, Eleanor, under the name The Similitudes. We had made tapes and sung in many towns the length and breadth of the country. Big rallies. Small rallies. Even on the continent . . . but no gig was ever as great as the one at which we sang in Croydon! Almost two years to the day. We'd just performed and as I wandered off the stage, the usual cacophony of slowly rising murmurings: 'Great night. Good, eh? Pub? Love your dress!' when there, twenty yards ahead of me (and walking away, I hasten to add) was Angie! All I saw was her back and her legs. Didn't need anything else. Back and legs! I couldn't believe my eyes. I ran after her and said something inane like 'Hello'.

I'd love to say that her expression was one of 'It's you! I thought I'd lost you for ever' and then collapse in my arms, but . . . not quite . . .

Her look was more of 'I know your face from somewhere, but who are you again?'

Thankfully, she eventually remembered and, without going into any more embarrassing details, I made a date. Specific this time with telephone numbers, full names and addresses, etc., etc. Forewarned was forearmed. (Just in case I should be confronted by any more Swastika-wearing ladies.)

This time, we were to meet behind Charing Cross Railway Station. Why there? I have no idea. It just seemed like a good idea at the time. I arrived early. But . . . some forty-five minutes later—no Angie! I thought, 'You great puddin'. You've been stood up!'

I can remember angrily pulling away sharply from the kerb and almost hitting a little maroon Mini. Obviously, I was quite cross: one, at being stood up; and two, by this Mini moron driver who was clearly driving far too fast! She gesticulated back and roared on . . . You got it—it was her! Angie. Equally as angry as me because she thought she'd been stood up as well; she'd been waiting in the wrong place. Or I had . . . ? What does it matter? It was her!

She hadn't seen me at that stage, but I managed to catch up with her at the lights and, using my very best police-gesticulation-method, I signalled her to pull in! Amazingly, she did! It had to be fate! Adding up all the probabilities; how did we actually meet up—nearly not—twice—given all the variables!

But that wasn't to be the end of it . . . It turned out that Carlisle United were playing a cup match against Leeds that afternoon that was to be on the radio. Carlisle United on the radio! Unheard of! The Cumbrian team which I'd supported since I was twelve—on the radio! Obviously it had meant a great sacrifice by yours truly to have arranged a date on such an auspicious day . . . but Angie liked Sniffer Clarke . . . who just happened to play for Leeds!

We spent a wonderful two-hour first date down by the Serpentine listening to a football match! And you don't think that was fate!?

A lot of water has gone under the bridge since that day. Almost fifty years, in fact, but she's always known how to keep my head turned her way and make me feel a million dollars into the bargain! Just walking down the street with her hanging on my arm still makes me feel great. She'd make blokes heads turn just by being there. She always looked wonderful, never like a sack of potatoes tied in the middle! I think I'd better stop before you stick your fingers down your throat! Suffice to say, I reckon I was, and am, a lucky fella!

But . . . there came the rub . . . What if things had gone the other way on OK Corral day? I suppose it started off more or less like any other day, dry and a little overcast, but the clouds were whisping and curling like witches' fingers preparing to cast their diabolical spells. I should have taken notice. I arrived at work in plenty of time for my shift and was about to don my motorcycle gear when the skipper shouted, 'John! Bob! Got a job for you.'

Getting my priorities right, I first put the kettle on before wending my way to the sergeant's office, where I found Bob had already arrived and was chatting to Bert, our shift sergeant.

'Big hush-hush job just come in and two drivers needed,' said Bert. 'So hush-hush that they won't even tell me what it's about! Apparently CID Serious Crime Squad want two drivers to collect two vans and meet them at HQ for a briefing at 1600.'

Sounded exciting but very mysterious. It wasn't often that traffic mixed with CID, let alone the serious crime squad! Intrigued, we took the solos up to the garage where we collected the two vans. (Not before downing our cups of tea, of course!)

On our arrival at HQ we were quickly ushered into the squad office where we found twenty or thirty plain clothes guys lounging around waiting for the powers that be to arrive with the plans for whatever was to ensue. The more questions we asked the more we realised no one had a clue what was going on! Eventually, silence descended on the gathered few, as three guys arrived with files under both arms. The room was plunged into darkness and the OHP was lit up.

'This job has been eight months in the planning,' boomed a voice from the back, 'and we want no cock-ups now. So listen carefully.'

'We received information some time back,' started another voice, 'about a Group 4 heist.'

'Information was received,' started yet another voice, 'that one of the top SE London gangs were to target a bullion load in transit by Group 4.

'An intensive surveillance exercise was, and still is, being carried out by several of our undercover officers from both within and without of the gang targeted, resulting in today's exercise.'

'Needless to say, everything is on a need-to-know basis, but each of you will know exactly what to do, when to do it, and what will be required of you at each stage of today's ongoing job. But when we say, "Keep your heads down," we mean, "Keep your heads down!" Bullets are gonna fly and we don't want anybody to end up with two arseholes!'

He got the message over, and the preamble continued. Apart from the three voices, you could have heard a pin drop. No doubt several of those present had been involved in similar exercises as this, but being all new to Bob and I, we were held spellbound. We knew that for this sort of job to be successful, undercover officers had to infiltrate the gangs concerned at extreme cost to themselves and their families, and, with not a little danger. Meticulous organisation was required, mingled with total trust for, and in, each other's abilities. One loose word or action could mean serious consequences for the undercover guys.

This job had, by all accounts, gone well and was just about to resolve itself with, hopefully, numerous arrests and several big-time hoodlums being taken off the street. What was to happen, as far as we could discern, was that a Group 4 van was to be attacked somewhere on its daily route, and Bob and I were to drive two vans back. As they said, 'You'll know all you need to know about what to do and when to do it!' Surely, they could give us a bit more? But no. That was it. In other words, 'Keep out of the way and just drive the two vans back.' As it turned out, I think we'd ahve been bricking it had we fully known what was to transpire!

We were to take the vans to a given location and then secrete ourselves in nearby bushes until called. At no time were we to leave our hideout, regardless of what transpired, until told to do so.

We were secreted (i.e. in the bushes!) at 1730 hours awaiting whatever was about to happen at 1800 hours.

I have been in more comfortable places, it has to be said. The bushes turned out to be holly bushes which, once inside, was fine, but getting into them was another story. Holly bushes always seem to have a thick overcoat with next to nothing underneath, the older they get, the thicker the coat and emptier the inside, these were ancient hence their internal void was a great hiding place. We were totally hidden from passersby, but the time dragged. We couldn't sit or move much. The ants were intrigued with two pairs of size tens disturbing their homes, and even more intrigued as several of their mates got squashed in front of their eyes as they attempted to clime hairy poles!

However, the word came, 'Three minutes to action.' Ants were forgotten as we waited enthralled for the 'action'. The road was clearly visible in front of us with unrestricted views to both left and right. Not a soul was in sight, not even any of the guys from the briefing.

As we watched we became aware of a flatbed lorry coming towards us and a Group 4 van thirty to forty yards behind it. The Group 4 van was more a box lorry than a van, with the typically heavily wired windscreen and side windows. As the flat bed passed our position, it suddenly braked, severely, and was rammed into reverse.

For the first time I became aware of a motorised crane following the Group 4 van. The jib of the crane was lowered in front of it and for all the world looked like some freakish jouster with his lance extended ready to poke some poor contestant unmercifully in the shield, or in these circumstances, severely in the back doors of the Group 4 van! The timing of the gang was perfect.

As the rear of the flatbed connected with the front of the Group 4 van, totally halting its forward motion, so the crane jib hit its rear doors. With an ear-splitting crash, the doors burst open.

What the gang were expecting at that point certainly didn't happen as out spilled what I assumed were CID men, fully armed. One of the men in the crane must have lost his bottle and fired a gun. That was enough for Bob and me as we fell flat to the floor. For a while it sounded like the Wild West, as gunfire was exchanged for what was only a few seconds but felt like many minutes.

'Okay! Okay! Okay!' shouted a voice and all firing stopped.

When Bob and I deigned to rise from the damp soil, dry holly leaves and the legion of ants, we were just in time to see five men being led away in handcuffs. Surprisingly, there were no bodies. Whether that was because everyone had been lousy shots or there just hadn't been as much shooting as we'd thought, I don't know, but it appeared to have been a smooth, injury-free exercise with a perfect outcome.

Now it was our turn, the five prisoners were loaded into the rear of our two vans . . . and we drove them back to the station. Bit of an anti-climax after all the 'warfare'!

All that was left for Bob and I to do was simply to search our specific vans, write a statement, and go home.

It was weird to leave 'bent' vehicles like that in the middle of the road. Normally that would have been our starting point and therefore our job to sort out. But weird and bent was a good way to put it. The poor old Group 4 van was like a dog with the back of a flatbed lorry in its mouth, and as for the crane . . . I can only leave it to your imagination where it was stuck!

We thought that was the end of it, at least as far as Bob and I were concerned (apart from repeating the saga round the canteen table, and repeating it with friends, with family, with more friends, round the canteen table again), and more or less left it, thinking it was all over. The bad guys would be locked up, feathers were put in multifarious hats, and the world could rest a little more at ease with these characters out of the way.

You can see why thoughts of my family were very much in the ascendant at this point. *What if*? Maybe it was time to think of pastures new . . . Could I leave all this behind?

However, twelve to eighteen months later, Bob and I were summoned to the Old Bailey to give evidence. What could they possibly want with us? We'd simply hidden in the bushes and driven the prisoners back! It was very rare to get called to the Old Bailey, particularly for traffic lads like us. Magistrates court—very often; sessions—often; but the Old Bailey . . . this was my one and only time!

I rose early, showered, splashed aftershave all over, donned my best uniform and was at the court bright and early ready to 'do battle' whatever that was. There were more wigs and gowns per square meter than acorns under our oak tree. Eventually the prosecution barrister came to us (the one on our side) looking very bright and breezy, yet sombre at the same time—must have been the wig—and reassured us that it was highly unlikely that we would be called, but that if we were it was simply to tell of our slight—very slight—involvement in the proceedings, basically the search of our vehicles. The search of our vehicles!

I could hardly remember the drive back, let alone the search of the vehicle! I'd only given it a cursory glance. The arresting officers had done most of that, hadn't they?

They'd climbed aboard, handcuffed to their prisoners and been with them all the time. What purpose would it serve, searching after they'd got out?

All I remembered was that my search had been brief. Very brief! But a slight snippet of information reaching me, as our barrister wandered off to the court room, was that 'a hammer had gone missing'!

A hammer had gone missing! A hammer had gone missing! Did the whole case revolve around that hammer? Had it been in my van, and I'd missed it? Would the whole case collapse because of a missing hammer? One that I'd missed. One that I'd missed because of a sloppy search? Months of intensive undercover work wasted because I couldn't be bothered to search my van properly. Lives put at risk needlessly because of me . . . I felt ill. The case was going to collapse because of me. I was going to look a fool, a lazy, incompetent fool. I was going to lose my job.

The loud speaker suddenly cut across my thoughts telling me to go to court room four. I needed to go to the loo. I wanted to be sick! Why hadn't I found that hammer? Why hadn't I searched properly?

By the time I entered the court room and made my way to the witness stand, I'd worked myself up to such a pitch that I could hardly climb the steps to face the judge!

The judge was even higher up. In an ultra-ornate 'hut'. Clad all in black and an even more ostentatious wig than our barrister had. All alone on his 'throne' in his own ornately carved box, staring at me!

Was that a black square he had on his head?

'What happened to the hammer? Why didn't you search your van properly?' I thought I heard him say. (He didn't, I just thought he did.) Actually he just smiled at me.

I read the oath 'I promise to tell the truth, the whole truth, and nothing but the truth.' I gave my name, number, and allocated work, and then waited to be questioned, at least I presumed I was to be questioned. It was what I'd done and said a thousand times before in all the other courts prior to giving evidence, but on all the other occasions, I knew I'd done my job properly. Today, at the Old Bailey, the highest court in the land, the court known throughout the world, I hadn't or didn't!

Our barrister asked me a question. I haven't a clue what it was as the room started to sway. A high-pitched whistle-cum-buzz assaulted my ears. The swaying started to darken. The whistling got louder . . .

I grabbed the rail in front of me, but my legs were turning to water. I no longer had control of anything as I heard the judge saying, 'Officer? Officer, are you alright?'

His words were like an echo in a cave. Each word rising and falling in volume and intensity. (It reminded me of the dentist chair when I was a kid having gas just before an extraction. Just before I fell asleep.) I knew nothing more until I found myself outside the courtroom with someone leaning over me and blowing a fan in my face! I felt horrendous. How I didn't vomit on the spot I don't know!

'You don't have to go back into court,' someone was telling me. 'The judge was happy for them to read your statement in lieu.'

I'd fainted in the witness box! At the Old Bailey!

It took several minutes to come round and for me to realise I'd made a complete plonker of myself. It's amazing how such nonsensical mayhem in your head can almost put you in the loonybin. It turned out that the hammer had been found in another vehicle and was nothing to do with me anyway.

I said the Old Bailey was the highest court in the land. Actually it wasn't, it was the High Court, followed by the Court of Appeal and finally the House of Lords. The House of Lords has now been replaced by the Supreme Court which is the final court of appeal in the UK for civil cases, and for criminal cases from England, Wales, and Northern Ireland and hear cases of the greatest public or constitutional importance affecting the whole population.

It would be more likely for me to find chickens' teeth than it would be for me to attend one of these courts!

Yet attend the High Court I did.

It all started one day at the Angel Islington, many years prior to my last story, I was riding my solo around North London, probably thinking of fish and chips or a day at the seaside with my family, or both, when a call came out 'Serious RTA at the Angel.'

RTA meant Road Traffic Accident and as there were no other takers . . . Off I went.

On my arrival, I found the usual pandemonium: cars, buses, and lorries everywhere, all trying to circumnavigate the accident, but there, half on the pavement and half in the roadway, with his leg under the rear wheels of an artic, was a pedal cyclist. Artic versus leg! Only one winner I'm afraid!

An ambulance had been called by a member of the public and one or two pedestrians made themselves known to me as witnesses to the incident. The lorry driver was obviously there too, and was, in many ways, in a worse state than the cyclist due to shock!

'I didn't see him,' the lorry driver groaned. 'Why do they come up the inside?' He was almost in tears as he attempted to keep it together. There was a café nearby and I suggested he got himself a cup of tea, while we waited for the ambulance.

It gave me time to talk to the cyclist, who was actually quite lucid and seemed to be almost past the pain barrier. I don't know how he was so calm; he only had a slight grimace on his face, but no more than you or I would have had if we simply got a splinter in the finger, bearing in mind his leg had just endured the weight of an artic trailer crossing his tib and fib!

'Can you tell me what happened?' I asked.

'The lorry was stationary at the lights and waiting to turn left, I think,' he whispered. 'His front wheels were turned slightly to the left and he must have been four to five feet away from the kerb. There was plenty of room for me to go up the inside and get away as soon as the lights changed.'

I don't know much about bikes, not being a cyclist myself, but I could see that his was a pretty fancy piece of kit, and very capable of getting away fast.

'What happened then?' I asked, giving him time to regroup.

'I got to the lights just as they were about to change, but not enough time to simply ride through. I put my foot down to keep balance, but it didn't land!'

'Didn't land?' I queried

'It was a weird feeling. I was expecting to touch the pavement, but it didn't and over I went!'

I was a little bemused but as I looked around, I saw a paving slab was missing from the footpath and a hole six inches to a foot deep was where it should have been. Upon later examination I found the slab leaning against the wall beside two traffic cones, but why the cones were not around the hole I never found out.

Witnesses later confirmed his story and said they had seen him put his foot right in the middle of the hole and lose his balance. One had had to shout up to the lorry driver to stop as he appeared to be completely unaware of what had transpired.

The lorry driver couldn't add any more and so, after making a few more enquiries around the area with regards to the 'non placement of cones', I completed my report and handed it in at the police station. I told the admin sergeant that it appeared to be a tragic accident with only the hole to blame (together with whomsoever had removed the cones or not put them there in the first place!).

I didn't think much more about it until some five—yes, *five*—years later when I was summoned to the High Court to give evidence. Needless to say, it took some time to get my head around the happenings of five years earlier, together with the fact that I was being summoned to the High Court!

What made this case worthy of that court?

You can imagine how 'poshed-up' I got for my attendance! I remember I even bulled my boots for the occasion. Something I hadn't done in many a long year. Not since my training school days in fact, when we were constantly on parade and being examined, from head to toe, normally by the parade sergeant (with his bad breath, nose to nose contact and eyes that burned deep into your soul!) or else for some dignitary or other visiting for the day—and heaven help the recruit who had the slightest blemish on his boots or no razor sharpness in his trouser creases! Well, I wouldn't be examined on my arrival at court, but I did want to look my best.

You can imagine my shock on being met at the door, called Mr Tinnion, rather than by my collar number, offered a cup of tea, introduced to the case barrister, ushered to my seat in the court, and informed I would be called soon!

I said earlier in the chapter that the higher the court, the better the treatment, well here I was proving it. Very different—very!

As the various barristers laid out their individual preambles, it became apparent that the injured pedal cyclist had just started a business when the accident occurred. Needless to say, the said business had been kept on hold for twelve months whilst his injuries improved. On rebooting the business, it had taken off and had become a million-pound concern! The cyclist was now suing somebody for not 'coning' the hole. His argument being that:

1. Had it been coned; he would not have put his foot down at that point.

2. He would therefore not have fallen off.

3. He would not have sustained the injury which had 'frozen' his business.

4. He now wanted the compound value of the business had it not been frozen (i.e. what it would have been worth had it traded for that lost year).

That was basically what the barristers' preambles were about, but whereas it has taken me a paragraph to write, it took them hour and a half to say! Well they were talking in Monopoly numbers!

I must admit, I found it fascinating and not at all boring, but suddenly, in one of the barristers' mid-flows, the judge lifted a book and slammed it hard onto his desk. I nearly jumped out of my skin; goodness only knows what it did to the barristers; but a complete hush fell on the courtroom.

'Mr Bloggs,'—or whatever the barristers name was—'I have an officer sitting at the rear of this courtroom, who has left his extremely important business of protecting this land and who is not in the slightest bit interested in your submissions. Kindly call him forthwith and let's allow him to return to his work!'

The hush continued for a moment and then a very red-faced barrister pushed his specks back up a very damp, dare I say sweaty, nose, and said, 'Please call Officer Tinnion to the stand!'

It took a moment for me to realise that the officer of whom the judge had spoken . . . was me. If it is possible to feel sheepish and twenty feet tall at the same time, then that was me.

As I climbed into the box, the judge continued, 'Officer, please accept my most sincere apologies on behalf of the court for your wait, and once again I am dreadfully sorry to have had to put you through those foregoing submissions. Please take the oath. Thank you.'

I hadn't a clue what to say except, 'Thank you, sir.' It felt very lame but as the judge was now firmly ensconced in note taking, I took the oath and gave my evidence.

When finished, the judge again looked at me and said, 'I am most obliged to you, Officer, thank you. You may now leave the court room.'

And with that—I left.

I just wish that my previous umpteen court appearances, and my umpteen appearances to come, had been and were to be, like that!

Chapter Twenty-One
Now What?

It's difficult knowing where to stop when you start writing mini stories like this—so many to tell—fantastic for me to recall—maybe for you to read—maybe not!

The thing was, that once I entered the Traffic Division, stories came even thicker and faster; particularly when I became an advanced accident reconstructor (that was reconstructing the scenes of fatal accidents; trying to piece together how an accident had occurred from a simple skid mark on the road surface or the damage to a tree—or rather the indentation left to the front of a car by a tree). Complicated but so interesting. All of which made it more and more difficult for me to make the monumental decision: 'Should I Stay or Should I Go' as The Clash so aptly put it! I loved my job!

I remember on one occasion attending the scene of a fatal accident involving a HGV and a mum with a pram. As with the lorry and the pedal cyclist recalled earlier, there was only one winner, but who was to blame? That's where the accident investigator came in.

The circumstances of this incident in a nutshell were that traffic was very heavy, in fact it was rush hour, and the mum wanted to cross the road between the front of the lorry and the rear of a car. Everything was stationary when the woman stepped from the kerb pushing a push chair into the gap left between the two static vehicles. However, as is the want in these sorts of circumstances, traffic was just about to start moving again.

Mum realised the dilemma too late and as the lorry rumbled onto her, she managed to push the pushchair containing her baby hard away from her, saving her baby, but unable to save herself and her toddler. The lorry only moved a couple of car lengths before coming to another halt, regrettably having driven over them both.

The driver was totally unaware of what had transpired until a distraught passer-by screamed at him.

On my arrival, the crowd were all for lynching the lorry driver and were only being kept at bay by some stalwart work by foot duty officers already on scene.

'The moron must have seen her!' one witness said. 'She was right under his nose!'

'I reckon he was traffic-jam comatosed,' said another.

'If he wasn't drunk then he's on drugs, or has been driving way beyond his permitted hours! He couldn't have failed to see her.'

On and on went the observations of the roadside lawyers.

No-one spared a thought for the shocked and distraught lorry driver sitting in his locked cab with his head in his hands weeping.

Maybe he was to blame? Maybe he could have stopped had he seen her? And there laid the rub. Had he seen her?

He'd been tried, found guilty and sentenced by every witness at the scene, and yet he could only have been doing one or two miles per hour at the time of the occurrence, therefore, surely he would have stopped. Nobody in their right mind could drive on knowing what they'd done, or about to do.

There was only a few reasons for this tragedy. One, he'd been negligent (traffic-jam comatosed as one witness had said). Two, distracted for whatever reason. Or three, he really had not seen her. What was certain was that he had not done it deliberately!

'Hadn't seen her.' Was that possible? All facts pointed towards the contrary, he'd only been the thickness of a windscreen away from her, but that was why investigations had to be carried out at any fatal accident. What were the facts?

The foot duty officers completed an accident report while I was left to measure up; chat some more to witnesses; assess the situation and basically think about this horrendous accident. How could it possibly have happened other than negligence?

The scene was tidied up and the lorry taken to a garage for me to examine thoroughly. Upon further examination, I found the lorry to be in perfect order; all documentation was in order, including drivers' hours and everything was pointing towards negligence— until my six-foot mate walked in front of the cab!

Whilst sitting in the driver's seat, I happened to look up from my report just in time to see him walking from left to right in front of me. He had been visible through the nearside window, but as he traversed under the windscreen, only the crown of his head was visible until he emerged into view through my offside window. The top of his head, at six foot, was only just visible through the windscreen. What about a five-foot-five woman?

The lorry was parked in an open compound, and I asked Bob to go and stand in front of the cab again while I sat in the drivers' seat.

Sitting back and assuming the driving position, some three and a half feet from the windscreen, I looked out. I couldn't see him.

I shouted out of the window, 'Stand with your back to the lorry radiator grill and slowly walk forward.' As he did so, the top of his head slowly came into view. I shouted for him to stop and then measured his distance from the cab. Five feet! At six feet in height!

The woman had only been around five-foot-five tall and would have had to have been considerably farther away before the lorry driver would have been able to see her. There had only been around a three- to four-foot gap between the lorry and the car when the woman stepped out.

Engine noise, traffic noise, general hubbub of the London world would have blocked out any other sound in the cab. The lorry driver would have been oblivious to the lady with the push chair.

I did a similar exercise from the offside driver's door as well as the nearside passenger door. Both times, the distances amazed me, but from the passenger side, or nearside pavement side, Bob was over twenty feet away before his head came into view. The woman had stepped from the nearside pavement and would have been totally in the driver's blind spot.

Almost every lorry cab was designed the same way. Here was a serious visibility problem.

I completed my report, stating, in effect, that the lorry driver would not have been able to see the deceased lady at any point during the tragedy. Either when she stepped from the kerb or moving in front of the cab. I concluded that it was my considered opinion that here was a serious manufacturing issue that required immediate attention to avoid any further similar catastrophes.

Cases of this nature are horrendous and extremely upsetting for all concerned, including the police, but they required investigation to correctly apportion culpability.

Drivers would often say, 'The brakes failed,' 'The sun was in my eyes,' or 'I couldn't do anything about it.'

Well that was my job, to discover how it had happened? Accident investigation. A really rewarding episode in my life.

Epilogue

I am delighted with the cards I have been dealt in life. Great wife, my mentor and confidante. Great son, whom, as I have said, I class as one of my best mates. Great daughter, who has brought so much light into my and others' lives with her sporting prowess, her love, her sensitivity to people and situations (not forgetting the hours of fun she gave me with a red bobble spoon). My grandchildren are wonderful too, but also, life has woven a rich tapestry for me. I have never wished that I'd ever taken another turning at the many 'Y' junctions that came my way . . . and that's why I don't know where to stop in my narrative!

So many more stories. The second half of my police career, did I remain in the Met? My aid work in war torn Yugoslavia back in the nineties. Our charity work in Thailand . . . Where does one stop? At what point do life's short stories become a biography? I know as I've related some of my escapades to friends and so on and they've said I should put pen to paper.

About the Author

John is a proud Carlisle United-supporting Cumbrian who joined the Metropolitan Police in 1967 after a two-year body-bending Cadet Corps experience! These were days when the personal radio was unknown, and the blue police box was nothing to do with Dr Who!

John captivates the reader from the start with his down-to-earth style of writing-as-he-speaks. Stories range from his early police days in Walworth SE London to the excitement of high-octane life on the motorcycle and fast response cars as a Traffic Division officer. However, he has also led a hugely varied life, being involved in charity work in many parts of the world, from Thailand to India, Croatia to Uganda, as well as leadership of a house church in Malvern.

John is a family man, married to Angie since 1974. He has two children, Carl and Stacey, and five grandchildren, Alanah, Gabriel, Rhys, Myoriee and Elijah. He doesn't look old enough but they're a lovely, amazing bunch!